# LINCOLNSHIRE
## Heritage Walks

Danny Walsh

First published 2014

The History Press
The Mill, Brimscombe Port,
Stroud, Gloucestershire, GL5 2QG
www.thehistorypress.co.uk

British Library Cataloguing in Publication Data.
A catalogue record for this book is available from the British Library.

ISBN 978 0 7524 8277 4

Typesetting and origination by The History Press
Printed in Great Britain

# CONTENTS

# ACKNOWLEDGEMENTS

Most of this book is the result of much fine work carried out by countless individuals before me, all sharing an enthusiasm and passion for Lincolnshire's heritage that we seem to be able to keep to ourselves! These local amateur historians are due a huge amount of gratitude for opening our eyes to the wonders we have within our own county. And just in case anyone thinks Lincolnshire is boring, we need only cough politely and mutter under our breath the words 'Wolds' and 'cathedral'. So it is our local amateur historians, naturalists and archaeologists who deserve most of the credit here.

All images are part of the author's collection.

# INTRODUCTION

A love of walking and a passion for local heritage are perfect bedfellows, complementing each other perfectly. The purpose of this book is to get you out and about, 'in the field' as it were, and in Lincolnshire this has to be taken literally. Walking is by far the best way to connect with local heritage, natural and 'unnatural' history. It is seeing it in reality and getting a feel for what happened on the ground which gives us the excitement and feeling of connection with past lives and events. You simply can't get this from a history book. To stand where a soldier stood, and look around seeing the possible points of attack and viewpoints for defensive positions, or to tread the paths of the ancient farmer and feel how the lee of the woods would help the crops to grow, is to better understand history than reading about it. You will understand much more about Lincolnshire's wildlife, geology, farming, village history, customs and traditional culture by undertaking these treks and seeing it for yourself. Which is why of course you should not just read this book, you should take it for a walk!

The book cannot hope to go into enough detail regarding everything you will come across on the walks, but I hope it is sufficient to aid understanding and insight and also leave you wanting to dig a bit deeper. Along the way you will find enthusiasts who will be more than willing to offer you local stories and titbits. This is part of a long tradition of oral history, often sniffed at but in reality a goldmine of credible lived experience, of source material not to be instantly dismissed as gossip, but to be respected and learnt from. It could be a church volunteer serving you a cup of tea and tempting you to a piece of carrot cake against your better judgement. But a little indulgence will often go a long way. I have visited Horncastle many times looking for oddities from the antiques shops and ploughing hour upon hour through its second-hand bookshops, but I had never found time to look at the church. When I finally did, my visit was illuminated by a volunteer who served me the aforementioned cake. I learnt much of the history of the building and its people from her insight and enthusiasm.

I am – appropriately enough – beginning to ramble, so for information I have provided maps sufficient to allow you to plot the route on your map and thus find your way. Instructions like 'Turn left at the rotten tree stump just beyond the duck pond' deprive you of lessons in vital map-reading and route-finding skills. It's all part of the fun and means that I can't be blamed for the extra 5 miles you walked when you missed the tree stump. In this way you can deviate, lengthen or curtail the walks to suit your own needs too. But, be warned, though all mileages are fairly accurate, if it is wet or very hot the walk will be longer. A simple grading system is used, with one footstep being an easy route and five footsteps showing a good day out which will leave you 'fadged' and 'lobbing'! The book is also divided into four sections based upon the location of the walks. The bulk fall into the central 'Wolds' section, as is to be expected because of its wealth of natural beauty and heritage, while the other sections are 'Trent and Humber', 'The Wash and Fens' and 'The Roman South' between Lincoln and Stamford.

There is further reading included at the end of each chapter where relevant. This includes sources I have used and recommendations for taking your interest further. More importantly, however, I have included a 'Kids' Stuff' section for each walk and I hope this will prove to be both educationally sound and fun. There may be some preparation involved occasionally, but the more fun the walk, the more chance the youngsters will want to do it again.

**KEY**

Footprints indicate the difficulty of each walk, 1 being the easiest and 5 being the hardest.

# AN ECCLESIASTICAL CIRCUIT OF HORNCASTLE
## A Ten-Church Trail

## INTRODUCTION

This 17-mile walk circumnavigates Horncastle via eight villages, some of which are barely more than farmsteads. Each village has its own church, ranging from the redundant and dilapidated to the still very functional. Most of these churches are locked as a measure against vandalism, with entry being gained via a local keyholder. It is sad that I recently walked the route on the Sabbath and found only one open! I would particularly recommend that you prearrange access to Horncastle St Mary's, Scrivelsby and West Ashby, rather than risk them being shut. Apart from these superb churches, the interest lies in the Wolds scenery with its wildlife and farming heritage. The walk also makes a splendid dawn to dusk winter excursion, with plenty of hares and partridges to be seen. You will also get plenty of views of the Belmont television mast, which at 385 metres is the highest in the country.

## ROUTE

There is plenty of parking in Horncastle centre and from here you walk out south along the Viking Way and Horncastle Canal to Thornton Lodge Farm. There is parking here too, which is useful if you wanted to miss out Horncastle in order to take a whole day exploring its church, antique shops and bookshops. Then walk the route anticlockwise, coming back to the canal, before walking back into Horncastle. At 17 miles, the walk deserves a Grade 5.

Alternatively, the route can be split into two halves and done over two days and this is recommended if you wish to explore the insides of the churches. The first half starts as above but then follows the Viking Way

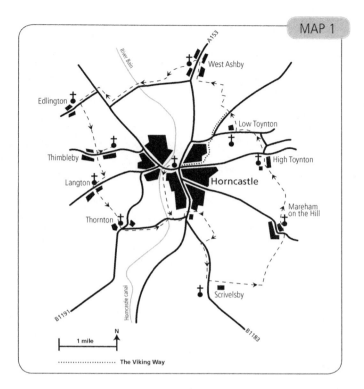

MAP 1

**MAP 1**

River Bain

A153

West Ashby

Edlington

Low Toynton

Thimbleby

High Toynton

Langton

Horncastle

Mareham
on the Hill

Thornton

Scrivelsby

B1191

Horncastle canal

B1183

N

1 mile

········· **The Viking Way**

back into Horncastle after Low Toynton (9 miles). The second day goes back up the Viking Way towards West Ashby and carries on anticlockwise back into Horncastle (9 miles).

## HORNCASTLE

Horncastle lies where the rivers Bain and Waring meet, and its name derives from the fact that it was on a horn-shaped piece of land which was once the site of a Roman fort or castle. The Roman township was called Banovallum and there are traces of Roman wall near the church.

In 1643, at the Battle of Winceby, Royalist Sir Ingram Hopton reputedly knocked Oliver Cromwell from his horse. When Hopton was killed, Cromwell had Hopton buried in St Mary's church in Horncastle out of respect for his

Dating back to 1250, St Mary's church was found to be infested with deathwatch beetles in its nave timbers in 2003. The beetles make a ticking sound, like a watch, which was once believed to be an omen of death.

prowess in battle. There are also a dozen scythe blades in the church which are said to have been used in the battle, though others suggest they are linked to the Lincolnshire Uprising of 1536.

St Mary's church is steeped in history. It has a low tower with what is called a candle-snuffer beacon, a rather poor apology for a spire! It is built of local sandstone and is restored with what Lincolnshire writers Yates and Thorold describe as an 'ugly' chancel arch. I thought it quite nice. The north wall has a worn brass of Sir Lionel Dymoke wearing his armour (knighted by Henry VIII after the Siege of Tournai and died 1519). It is said that a suit of armour belonging to Sir Lionel was taken from the church and used by one Philip Trotter, an insurgent in the Lincolnshire Rebellion (which Henry ruthlessly quashed). Another, even more worn, brass on the floor depicts Sir Lionel in a shroud.

Go to the altar and look to your left: you will see a tiny hole in the wall protected by an iron grille. Originally this was the outer wall of the church and these openings allowed the diseased and undesirable to see the altar and the service without infecting others. The Black Death or plague was rife in this part of Lincolnshire, wiping out entire villages, so the 'squint' served a very real purpose. Notice too the ten gilded angels in the nave and look for the green man above you! The church is open most Saturday mornings and as often as possible in summer, depending on volunteers.

Along with a market, the biggest horse fair in England used to be held in Horncastle every August since 1229, when the town was granted its market charter by Henry III. In its eighteenth-century heyday thousands of horses swapped hands, but the last fair was held in 1948. A plaque on Lloyds bank commemorates the fair.

Also note the miniature Albert Memorial, a monument to Edward Stanhope MP who represented Horncastle until his death in 1893. Look out, too, for the house in Bank Street sporting a blue plaque. The house once belonged to Sir Joseph Banks, the famous botanist, who sailed with Captain Cook on the *Endeavour* to Australia.

## Horncastle's Hangman

There is a tiny building in Church Lane which used to be a cobblers and home to one William Marwood. As well as being a cobbler, Marwood was a hangman and the public executioner from 1872 to 1883. Experimenting with sacks of corn, he perfected the more humane 'long drop' method of hanging. This involved dropping the prisoner through a trapdoor which would (if you had calculated the body weight and length of rope correctly) render the prisoner senseless, often breaking the neck, so that they suffered their death painlessly. Part of his technique was to place the noose's knot under the left ear! He travelled to prisons all over the country and was reputedly paid £10 a hanging. One perk of the job was that he got to keep the dead man's clothes and, in all, he executed 176 people. He succumbed to pneumonia at the age of 65. A devout Methodist with an alleged fondness for gin, he is buried in Holy Trinity churchyard in an unmarked grave because souvenir hunters chipped bits off his headstone until there was nothing left. The church is now an antiques centre.

## Horncastle Canal

This was originally a part of the River Waring and had much to do with Horncastle's growth in the Victorian era. It was completed in 1802 and was used for carrying wool, coal, grain and other goods. The coming of the railways heralded its demise and it was closed in 1871, but it had helped to double Horncastle's population. This canal leads us south out of Horncastle before turning east to cross the old River Bain, then south again to Scrivelsby. Take care on the small road section here.

# SCRIVELSBY

At the entrance to Scrivelsby Park are two lodges attributed to Humphry Repton, and an arched gateway, built in 1530. This is all that remains of the original Scrivelsby Court. Atop the arch is the 'Scrivelsby Lion' which is said to symbolise the office of 'King's Champion'.

Scrivelsby was the home of Robert Dymoke (pronounced Dimmock), hereditary Grand Champion to Richard III, Henry VII and Henry VIII. This right was originally granted to the lord of the manor at Scrivelsby by William the Conqueror. The role of the king's champion involved riding fully armoured into Westminster Hall (mid banquet!) on a white steed, throwing down your gauntlet and challenging to mortal combat anyone who questioned the king's right to succeed. The king would then drink from a gold wine cup and hand it to the champion, who drank from it, shouting 'Long live the King' and withdraw gracefully backwards ... or so

it goes. The champion was then rewarded with the cup. This happened for the last time at the coronation of George IV in 1821 and these days the champion just carries the standard of England at the coronation.

The largely Victorian church has many monuments to past champions, such as the Marmions (the original champion family) and the Dymokes (who succeeded them). Robert Dymoke has a tomb with a brass effigy on the lid and another Dymoke, Lewis, died in 1760 at the age of 90, a rare feat for those days. (Key available locally.)

Children will enjoy this section of the walk through the park with its herd of fallow deer and inquisitive sheep. Leaving the park, you follow a lane upwards towards Mareham on the Hill.

## MAREHAM ON THE HILL

Here you find a largely Georgian, but once medieval, church which does not look like a church at first glance. Inside it has some striking blue painted box pews, not to mention a double-decker pulpit! It's a peaceful spot and the churchyard is excellent for wild flowers in the spring.

## HIGH TOYNTON

High Toynton has the happy distinction of being the only village in Lincolnshire whose young men all came back from the First World War alive. The church, dedicated to St John the Baptist and originally thirteenth

# Kids' Stuff

**DRAW:**
One of the churches
An angel
A sheep
An item from William Drewry's gravestone

**MAKE:**
**A twig tower.** When in a wooded bit of the walk, find a spot with plenty of dead wood and try to build a tower. This gets a bit like playing Jenga in reverse, as you are adding things rather than taking them away. See how high you can make your tower without it toppling and leave it for others to marvel at and try to beat.

**PLAY:**
**A game of hangman.** In memory of Willam Marwood, use people, places and objects from this chapter and things you have seen on the walk. One game every rest stop.

**Walking bingo.** Design a bingo card (4x4) for each child with these things written in the squares: a king's head, market cross, spire, rook, mud and stud building, hare, scarecrow, partridge, brass monument, William Drewry's grave, a Durham ox, ivy, sheep, green man, bridge and lion. Prizes for all corners, a line and a full house.

**DECIDE:**
In St Mary's church, Horncastle, is Chancel Arch ugly or nice? Take a vote.

**LOOK UP:**
Candle snuffer
The long drop
Box pew
Hagioscope
The Battle of Winceby
Fallow deer

century, was restored in 1872. It is an impressive, solid building with a fine vaulted ceiling, just crying out to be used more.

## LOW TOYNTON

Just 1 mile further away down the lane, you wander into Low Toynton. Blink and you'll miss it. Redundant, sold into private ownership and now derelict, the church, dedicated to St Peter, was described by Yates and Thorold as 'not very interesting', but they tantalisingly added that it had a font with 'curious' designs. A real shame that we let our heritage disappear like this; it was a Grade II listed building and scheduled monument.

## WEST ASHBY

West Ashby has grown up along the road between Horncastle and Louth, which is now the busy A153. All Saint's church is the most prominent feature here, dating back to the thirteenth century, but it has been extensively restored. Inside there are a series of memorial tablets, including one to a Royal Navy Midshipman Richard Calthrop, who had the misfortune to get his head blown off in 1816. The tablet goes into some detail and is a grisly reminder of the dangers of naval warfare.

Outside is an interesting gravestone for William Drewry (died 1801). He was a freemason and his headstone depicts an hourglass, a scythe, and an arrow (all symbols of death). Above these is the Masonic symbol of the all-seeing eye – the sun.

From here the trail moves south-west towards Thimbleby, passing Thimbleby Mill and crossing the busy A158 Lincoln–Skegness road.

## THIMBLEBY

Thimbleby was called Stimbelbi in Domesday Book, when the lord of the manor was King William I. It has some fine mud and stud cottages apparently built by William Laxon, who built the first houses in North America. He sailed with Captain John Smith and was one of the original settlers in Jamestown, Virginia in 1607. St Margaret's church was restored in 1879 and looks stunning from along the street. It is a chunky building currently undergoing some badly needed restoration. There is also an old village pump dating back to 1857. A short hop across the fields will bring you to Langton.

## LANGTON

As you enter Langton, look out for a tiny old cottage with a corrugated-iron roof that looks like an old chapel. Langton was once essentially just a tiny farmstead of manor house, farm and this small towerless church, which has unusual pink and green glass.

## THORNTON

Snuggled cosily in the centre of the village, this church only consists of a nave and chancel and boasts locally made early nineteenth-century wrought-iron hat pegs, a quirky claim to fame perhaps. It is a haven of peace and nearly always open, so is a welcome rest before the home run back into Horncastle. From Thornton head back east to the canal and up into Horncastle for ...

## A WELL-EARNED PINT

The Kings Head is the only mud and stud building left in Horncastle, but do take the time to appreciate it from the inside!

_Further Reading_

Yates, J. and H. Thorold, _Lincolnshire: A Shell Guide_ (Faber and Faber: London, 1965)
community.lincolnshire.gov.uk/BolingbrokeCastle

# LOUTH, HUBBARDS HILLS AND BEYOND

This 8-mile walk starts from the Cathedral of the Wolds, St James' church, in the Capital of the Wolds, Louth. It takes in the local beauty spot of Hubbards Hills and then ventures out into the Wolds via Raithby and Hallington with classic views of St James' spire dominating the skyline. The walk then goes through the pleasant Welton Vale to South Elkington, before returning along good paths to Louth. There is much history and wildlife to be discovered along the route as well as the opportunity to explore several interesting churches. With a couple of small hills and a bit muddy in parts, the walk is a Grade 3. There is plenty of parking in Louth.

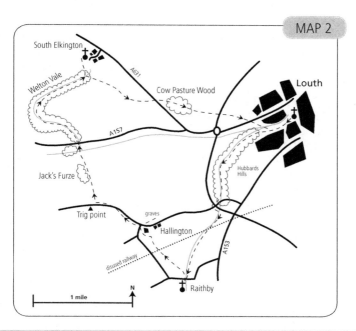

MAP 2

South Elkington
Welton Vale
A631
Cow Pasture Wood
Louth
A157
Jack's Furze
Hubbards Hills
Trig point
graves
Hallington
disused railway
A153
1 mile
N
Raithby

# LOUTH

There isn't space within this book to do justice to all that there is to see in Louth, and indeed it is such a fine town that it deserves a day of exploring to itself. The main streets such as Mercer Row, Westgate and the Market Square still teem with character and are littered with fine Georgian, Regency and Victorian buildings. In the eighteenth century, Louth was a place of high society with many balls and masquerades arranged by the local gentry, leading Barley to state in 1952 that such patronage gave Louth, 'a grace and polish not always seen in a secluded market town'. As with most towns, modern shop fronts have done little to add to the visual appeal of the streets, but look above the shop fronts and you have an architectural feast with the upper storeys left largely as they were. Louth's wealth was drawn from the wool trade and boosted by the opening of the Louth Navigation Canal in 1770 which brought many more trading opportunities. The current department store, Eve & Ranshaw, has a history dating back to 1781.

You will notice that many street names end in 'gate', which is Danish and means 'way' or 'road'. In Eastgate there is a plaque on a shop wall and the pavement informing you that you are standing on the Greenwich Meridian, 0 degrees longitude. Here you can stand with one foot in the east and one in the west, bridging the line which runs around the earth from pole to pole.

Another plaque in the corner of a former mill on Bridge Street recalls a tragedy, as it marks the level of the waters at the height of the Louth flood on 29 May 1920. Torrential rain in the Wolds drained through Hubbards Hills that afternoon, swelling the River Lud, the waters rising over 15 feet in half an hour. By that evening, the waters had destroyed many houses and twenty-three people lost their lives, with many others only able to save themselves by climbing onto their roofs. In the thick of the disaster a local doctor, W. Higgins, was called to a confinement. As he dealt with the patient upstairs, the waters crashed into the lower storey. The water rose and soon covered the bedroom floor and crept up to the mattress upon which the poor woman lay. Her husband leapt out into the torrent to get help, forgetting that he could not swim. The doctor leapt after him, saved him and then promptly delivered him a daughter. The doctor then escaped and arranged their rescue and went on to rescue five children. When he finally reached home, he was to find that it too had been devastated by the flood. In the days following, the Ministry for Health supplied 400 army huts to house the homeless.

The museum houses a replica of a 360-degree panorama of Louth, from the church tower drawn by William Brown in 1844. This shows you what the streets and landscape were like in and around the town as far out as

> When the plague struck (again) in 1631, the town was all but abandoned. Nobody would even dare touch money (that could have been handled by someone diseased) until it had been washed in vinegar!

the Humber and North Sea. The original oil paintings are hung in the town hall. The museum also has some fine examples of woodcarving by Thomas Wallis, alongside excellent displays.

The King Edward VI Grammar School in Edward Street boasts former pupils Alfred Lord Tennyson, Captain John Smith (of Pocahontas fame) and Sir John Franklin (of the North-West Passage fame). The school seal of 1552 shows a teacher birching a boy with the Latin inscription 'Who spares the rod, loves not his son'! One begins now to understand why Tennyson hated it here so much.

## ST JAMES' CHURCH

The jewel in Louth's crown is, without doubt, St James' church. The spire, often considered the finest in England, pinpoints Louth as you approach it from all sides and its sight from a distance is one of the finest Wold views. The church was finished in 1441 with just the tower, but it was not until 1515 that the spire was finished.

At 295 feet high, it is taller than the towers of Lincoln Cathedral and the tallest parish church in England. The weathercock was made from a copper basin taken from the Scots as part of the spoils from the Battle of Flodden. Climbing the spire seems to have been a local dare at one time, the last reputed attempt being in 1818 when (after drinking ten pints in the Wheatsheaf) a certain Mr Smith did so, tied a handkerchief around the weathercock and danced a jig to the horror of those watching from below ... or so it goes! The tower is often open to the public, to save you the necessity of risking life and limb, and the views from the top are stupendous. Wide panoramas, as painted by Brown, appear in every direction and one can look down on the day-to-day life of the town and marvel at its appearance like a model village. It is great fun trying to pick out landmarks on the horizon and recognise the places you have been down below.

The church itself is a fine example of perpendicular gothic architecture, but was considerably renovated in the 1860s by local architect James Fowler, also five times the town mayor. Yates and Thorold considered this somewhat a desecration. 'The church is an empty shell', they wrote, describing it as undistinguished and blaming Fowler for altering many north Lincolnshire churches 'to his own taste and that of his time'.

They were similarly caustic about the town hall, 'whose front looks like an annexe to the Vatican but whose back is more like a slaughterhouse'. Yates and Thorold may have overstated their case here, as the church contains much of interest and is quite beautiful. It is dedicated to St James, the patron saint of pilgrims, and a church has stood on this spot for over 1,000 years.

## HUBBARDS HILLS

This park is a beautiful wooded valley with the River Lud flowing through it and was created by glaciers around 70,000 years ago, give or take a few days. On a warm summer's day it is packed with families picnicking and paddling. It was gifted to the town in memory of his wife by the trustees of the estate of one Auguste Alphonse Pahud, a Swiss who used to teach French and German at the grammar school. In winter there is a fine higher-level walk amongst the beech trees clinging to the valley side and this is a good time to see finches, nuthatches and other woodland birds.

GAVE ALSO UNTO HER HUSBAND

JOHN AND ELIZABETH NESBITT

## THORPE HALL

Just up on the hill, to the right as you walk through the valley, is Thorpe Hall, unfortunately hidden from view. This was built by Sir John Bolle in 1584. He fought at Cadiz in 1596 and was knighted for his efforts and bravery. During the raid on Spain one Donna Leonora, a Spanish princess,

The vicar of Louth, Thomas Kendall, was hanged, drawn and quartered at Tyburn for his part in the Lincolnshire Uprising and many of the other ringleaders were hanged and displayed in Louth market square.

# Kids' Stuff

**FIND:**

The pulpit, with eleven carved apostles by the Louth craftsman T.W. Wallis. The twelfth apostle, Judas, appears only as a face in the stone foliage below.

Wallis' carvings of animals on the 'corporation' pews at the front.

Two modern carved heads outside on the south-aisle window, that of the canon and verger, immortalised during repairs in 1960.

The Louth imps, in between the windows of the second story of the tower.

The nave roof with its carved angels.

The rabbits in the window behind the organ.

The head of J. Fowler, the architect, carved by Wallis near the organ in the choir stalls.

Two original oak medieval roof angels in the Angel Chapel.

The Adam and Eve window.

Look up in the centre of the tower to see the ceiling. The sun, 86 feet above you, is the trapdoor from the bell-ringing chamber above it! Try to spot the beagle which peers down at you here too.

became his prisoner and she fell in love with him. (Another version has it that he was the prisoner!) Anyhow, being a true English gentleman, he remained faithful to his wife (or so we are told). The princess later sent him a portrait of herself in a green dress as a memento and left for a nunnery, to die broken-hearted. Today the house and grounds are said to be haunted by a Green Lady and she is most often seen gliding across the road by the hall. Another story has it that a place is set for her ghost at each mealtime in the hall.

Between Hubbards Hills and Raithby, you cross the disused railway line which ran from Louth to Bardney and then on to Lincoln. It included a tunnel under the Bluestone Heath Road near Stenigot. The path from Hubbards Hills as it nears Raithby is close to the source of the River Lud and is a good place to spot kingfishers.

## RAITHBY

Prettily set amongst the trees and streams, the church of St Peter, with its eight-pinnacled tower, has a lead-lined thirteenth-century font and was apparently wonderfully Gothic at its height.

It still has some grotesque corbels and its box pews remain, but much has been removed. Note the clarity of the chalk stream and springs here and, taking the path out of Raithby north towards Hallington, across the same stile you crossed coming in, notice the medieval village site where ancient streets and house platforms remain clearly visible.

## HALLINGTON

Before we reach Hallington we pass Station House, which was the village railway station until it closed in 1956. The village is recorded in Domesday Book as Halitun and having fifteen houses. It is likely that it was a medieval settlement with aerial photographs indicating the presence of ridge and furrow marks, the result of medieval ploughing. The parish church is long gone and all that remains here are three lonely graves.

Just east of Hallington is a place consisting only of a couple of houses called 'Pokes Hole', which means 'lost village'. On our road out of Hallington you reach a trig (triangulation) point indicating that you are at 111 metres above sea level. This is known as Hallington Top and is a good vantage point.

Turn around here and go back a few yards to the permissive footpath on your left. From here there is a fine view of the spire of Louth church. The route follows this path down to the busy A15 Lincoln–Louth road which you cross, so take care with the traffic.

# Kids' Stuff

**DRAW:**

**A stained-glass window.** Whilst you are in St James' church look at the lovely windows and design your own, then when you get back home try and make it out of black card and coloured tissue paper.

**MAKE:**

**A walk necklace!** As you are walking around collect some small but interesting natural objects and tie them together with some strong cotton. Then tie a long loop and wear it as a necklace.

**Your own ghost story!** The phantom of Hubbards Hills maybe?

**FIND:**
**The Elkington beasts!**

**LOOK UP:**
Turnpike trusts
Triangulation point

**FUN FACT**

A piece of Lincolnshire dialect is the old Lincs word, 'fluther-gullion'. This means a person who has a lot to say about nothing as in 'He's a right fluther-gullion'.

## WELTON VALE

A welcome retreat from the road, this planted ravine has a variety of both deciduous and coniferous trees. Look out for typical woodland birds here such as long-tailed tits and treecreepers and notice the Giant Californian Redwood trees and again the quality of the chalk stream. Near the top of the vale you pass a rather worn whale bone arc, once the entrance to Elkington Hall. There is a quarry nearby which is a Site of Special Scientific Interest and has important Ice Age deposits. Here have been found prehistoric hand axes made from flint, alongside the remains of giant deer and elephants. The area was quarried for sand and gravel and provided material for runways in the Second World War. As you near the top of the vale, watch out for the path to South Elkington: it is a left-hand branch over a small bridge and onto a boardwalk.

## SOUTH ELKINGTON

All Saints church has a south arcade dating from 1209 with the tower, font and roof constructed in the fifteenth century. The rest was restored by Fowler in 1873. Notice the painted chancel ceiling depicting the twelve apostles and the carved beasts on the bench ends in the choir.

The church overlooks the village and is a fine place for a breather surrounded by trees. It was not always such a peaceful spot. Toll gates set up here in the early 1800s by the local Turnpike Trust to raise funds to keep the roads in good repair were frequently broken down by locals who refused to pay the tolls and resented the new barriers across their traditional routes. Take care crossing the A16 Louth bypass as you near Louth.

Our walk re-enters Louth via Westgate and we are again greeted by wonderful views of the spire and of the Wheatsheaf, a strong contender for the best pub in the book and certainly an excellent place to finish this walk. It was a coaching inn built in 1625 and retains much of its character – feeling like a pub ought to feel!

*Further Reading*

Barley, M.W., *Lincolnshire and the Fens* (Batsford; London, 1952)

Bourne, J.K., 'The Louth Weathercock' in *Lincolnshire Life*

Bourne, J.K., 'The Louth Flood' in *Lincolnshire Life*

Codd, D., *Haunted Lincolnshire* (Tempus Publishing Ltd; Stroud, 2006)

Martineau, H.D. 'A Cameo of Louth' in *Lincolnshire Life*

Robinson, D.N., 'The Story of Hubbards Hills' in *Lincolnshire Life*

Yates, J. and H. Thorold, *Lincolnshire: A Shell Guide* (Faber and Faber; London, 1965)

# THE BELCHFORD CHALLENGE WALK!

MAP 3

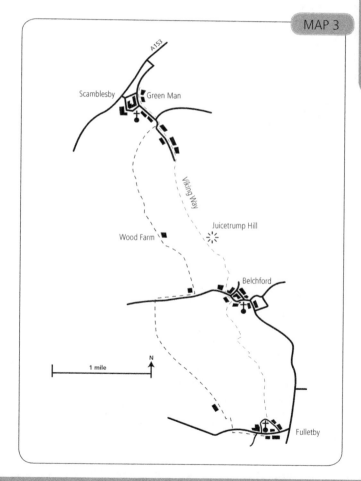

This is a walk of two halves which can be joined together as a figure of eight to create a longer walk of 9 miles. The walk is centred on the unfortunately named Belchford, whose church was at the centre of the 1536 Lincolnshire Uprising. The route goes both north and south of Belchford in two circles to Scamblesby in the north (5½ miles) and Fulletby to the south (4½ miles). Half of the route is along the Viking Way and takes in history, churches, archaeology and wildlife. The challenge relates to the annual Belchford Downhill race for homemade go-carts, an example of Lincolnshire's more modern cultural heritage. Parking is available next to the church in Belchford. At Grade 2 there are a few low hills but no real difficulties, with the path being well defined throughout.

## ROUTE 1: THE SCAMBLESBY LOOP

### Belchford

Belchford lies on the Viking Way and is famous for being at the centre of the Lincolnshire Uprising, following the dissolution of Louth Park Abbey in 1536. Belchford church tells the tale of the protest against Henry VIII's closure of the monasteries and impending inquisition of the clergy. The locals, including many nobility and clergy, were worried about increased taxes on sheep, the seizing of church jewels and the closing down of their churches. Tensions reached fever pitch and there were mob lynchings and murders before 3,000 or so people gathered at Horncastle to protest and march upon Lincoln. Gathering from across Lincolnshire, their numbers had swelled to around 30,000 by the time they reached their destination. Here they occupied the cathedral and negotiations were held, but when news came through that the king's answer was a clear rejection of their demands and forces were on their way to suppress the uprising, things basically fizzled out. One of the ringleaders was the Parson

of Belchford, Nicholas Leache and for his troubles he was hanged, drawn and quartered for treason at Tyburn. The uprising caused Henry VIII to call the rebels the 'rude commons of one of the most beastlie shires in the whole realm' and Lincolnshire a 'land of vipers and hotbed of sedition which stunk in his nostrils'. The locals were right to worry, as it wasn't long before the churches were relieved of their riches.

The church of St Peter and St Paul was last rebuilt in 1783 but there has been a church on this site from 1153. However, the churchwarden had to sell the lead from the roof and two bells from the previous church to fund the rebuilding. It is built typically of green sandstone and has a nice fifteenth-century octagonal font, but most of the tower was taken down in 1902 to build the vestry. It is a good place to sit and rest and has some interesting gravestones in the churchyard.

## The Belchford Challenge

One of Lincolnshire's more bizarre cultural traditions is the annual Belchford Downhill Challenge. It is a race of homemade, gravity-propelled go-carts of all shapes and sizes, which come teetering (or Belching) down the hill and, should the brakes fail, crashing to a stop at the strategically placed hay bales at the bottom. This is a great local custom not to be missed, so time the walk to coincide with race day. Races start early and occur throughout the day and there are stalls and refreshments as well as a fantastic atmosphere.

The route leaves Belchford, west past the Bluebell Inn, and takes the track on the right called Sandy Lane. It will lead you over farmland, some of which has been turned into a wildlife area with ponds. There were many Neolithic and Roman settlements in this area so look for ancient field boundaries and earthworks along this stretch. When you reach a crossroads take the right-hand path down into Scamblesby.

## Scamblesby

Scamblesby's St Martin's church was rebuilt in the 1890s and is beautifully set amongst the trees down a quiet lane. It has a bell turret, Norman font and some beautifully carved poppy heads at the ends of the benches. Before heading back towards Belchford be sure to visit The Green Man pub, which was once a coaching inn.

The route back to Belchford is along a very pleasant section of the Viking Way, past Belchford Wood which is a good spot for bluebells in the spring. The path then runs past Juicetrump Hill and later takes you over the beginnings of the River Waring, which eventually runs through Horncastle.

Juicetrump Hill used to be regarded as a Neolithic long barrow and it is easy to see why, from its position overlooking the valley and its shape.

However, it is really an outcrop of roachstone (a type of limestone) which, being harder than the surrounding rocks, has not weathered as much.

## ROUTE 2: THE FULLETBY LOOP

Leave Belchford along the same road as before and walk a quarter of a mile further on until you reach a footpath on the left. This is followed across the fields until you come out on the minor road, where you head left into Fulletby.

### Fulletby

You are virtually on the top of the Wolds here, as Fulletby at 137 metres is one of the highest villages in Lincolnshire, with views towards Salmonby, Tetford and the Wolds beyond. In the other direction, on clear days, you can see Lincoln Cathedral over 20 miles away. The village is charming and would have been even more so back in 1841, when all the cottages were built of mud and stud.

An extraordinary man called Henry Winn lived here. He was the parish clerk for seventy-six years, but also served as the village policeman, schoolteacher, taxman, churchwarden and he also looked after the poor of the parish. He was also a writer and poet and founded the village library with his own books. All this apparently didn't drain his energy as he had twenty-one children, who were all born in Winn Cottage, which can still be seen. This also functioned as the post office, village shop and grocer's store. Winn himself lived to the age of 98, but only four of his children survived to adulthood and all but a daughter are buried in the churchyard. His gravestone can be found in the churchyard.

The church of St Andrew, originally fourteenth century, is another lovely greenstone church which was rebuilt in 1705 and last restored in 1857. There are some excellent carved stone faces by the door and the churchyard is particularly good for wild flowers in late summer.

The route back is north along the Viking Way and just as you leave Fulletby notice the bumpy field. These are the remains of the medieval Fulletby. Keep looking left for the views of Lincoln Cathedral.

### Lapwings

If there was a claim to be the Lincolnshire bird, the lapwing would be a prime candidate; it is even the symbol of the Lincolnshire Wildlife Trust. Lapwings wheel over this walk's fields, displaying in the springtime. The male flies up at speed, pauses and then slips and slides and swerves down to the ground ... almost. Then he sweeps low across the ground and suddenly launches himself up again, all the while crying and screaming

# Kids' Stuff

**DRAW:**
A Green Man.

**A go-cart design.** Resolve to enter next year's challenge.

**DECIDE:**
A new name for Belchford.

**PLAY:**
Find a quiet spot (not too far from your parents), preferably in a wood or by some trees. Now close your eyes and listen. Really relax and see if you can identify the different sounds that you hear.

**TRY:**
**Speaking in Lincolnshire dialect.** Here are a few words to try:

grass = gress
wash = wesh
master = mester
lake = lairk
slow = slaw
louth = Luth
Horncastle = Urnc'sle (try asking for directions!)
hi there = ay up

Practise by saying 'ay up mester' to everybody you meet, but remember that there is a fine line between impressing somebody and offending them, so be prepared to run!

**LOOK UP:**
The Belchford Downhill Challenge
The Green Man
The Lincolnshire Wildlife Trust

'pee-ee-weet'. The great bird artist and lapwing studier, Eric Ennion, had it perfectly when he said the lapwing flies like a 'bird demented'! The local Lincolnshire name is pyewipe or peewit, which comes from its call.

Several theories abound as to how they got their other name of lapwing and if you cross a field in the breeding season you will witness one reason. If the birds have young nearby they will draw predators, such as yourself or foxes, away from the nest by flying around them and screaming to divert your attention. If you get very close to the eggs or young, the female runs off limping and dragging (lapping or flapping) one wing on the ground as if it were broken, thus enticing the fox to go after her as an easy meal and leave the young alone. A high-risk strategy, but one that seems to work.

The other possible reason for the name lapwing is that, in flight, they appear to lazily flop their wings in what could be described as a lopping or lapping motion.

Other wildlife to watch out for are barn owls and yellowhammers. If you do the walk in autumn you will see some glorious displays of poppies and in springtime keep an eye out too for hares chasing each other around the fields.

---

*Further Reading*

Campion, G. Edward, *Lincolnshire Dialects* (Richard Kay; Boston, 1976)
Ennion, A.E.R., *Field Study Books: The Lapwing* (Methuen; London, 1949)
Robinson, David N., 'The Lincolnshire Uprising of 1536', www.horncastleuk.com

# A DATE WITH MAVIS ENDERBY

An 11-mile Wolds circular beginning at Winceby, near the site of the 1643 battle, this route takes in Snipe Dales Country Park and the villages of Hagworthingham, and Mavis Enderby, probably the best-named village in Lincolnshire. It then takes in Raithby by Spilsby and Old Bolingbroke, home to the remains of John of Gaunt's castle, before climbing uphill back to Winceby, via Asgarby and Hameringham. The walk offers superb Wolds views, history and an abundance of wildlife. Park at the small Snipe Dales car park in Winceby. The walk is Grade 4 due to some hills, muddy and occasionally overgrown terrain, medium length and the need for good map-reading skills in parts.

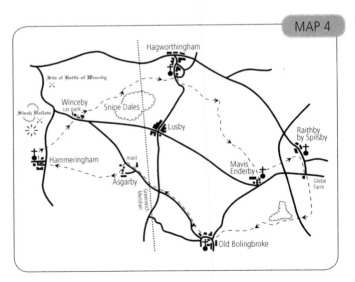

MAP 4

## WINCEBY

The Battle of Winceby took place on 11 October 1643, when Oliver Cromwell's Parliamentarians engaged Royalist troops who were coming to the aid of their besieged colleagues at Bolingbroke Castle. Though the battle lasted less than half an hour it was said to be one of the bloodiest of the English Civil War, with over 400 dying. The lane by the battle site is still called Slash Lane and the battle site itself is Slash Hollow. The battle was nearly Cromwell's last as he was knocked off his horse mid-battle and then dealt a blow by Sir Ingram Hopton, a local Royalist. However, Cromwell managed to mount another horse and continued the fray, urging his men on to victory. It was this decisive battle which helped to consolidate his reputation as a leader.

Winceby's church of St Margaret was rebuilt in 1866 when there were about seventy-eight locals, but as the congregation diminished, the church fell into disrepair and was demolished around 1964. There is still a path through the graveyard which is a peaceful spot to take a breather and contemplate the few gravestones left in evidence. Then head off through Snipe Dales.

## SNIPE DALES

This important nature reserve consists of steep-sided valleys where streams have cut through the Spilsby sandstone to the underlying Kimmeridge clay. In the valley bottoms, springs arise where the sandstone meets the clay to create wet flushes and streams perfect for the bird the reserve is named after. The flowers to look out for which are associated with these wetter areas are marsh marigold, yellow flag, lady's smock and ragged robin. Along the path note the green technology of the hydraulic ram, which uses pressure from the stream to take water to the nearby farm.

The adjoining country park also has a large area of coniferous woodland but this is being replaced with more and more native deciduous trees. So it is a good place for practicing tree identification. The trees also attract a good variety of birdlife which changes with the seasons. In winter it is a good place to try and lock on to a roving band of small birds as they move about the woods in mixed flocks foraging for food. Such flocks are likely to contain blue, great, long-tailed and coal tits, redpolls, siskins, goldcrests, treecreepers and finches. The last time I walked through I came face to face with an early morning badger doing its rounds. It looked me up and down, seemed to study me for a few moments, then waddled off in the opposite direction. You might not be so lucky, but you will come across many badger setts on this walk. Our route from here leaves the reserve and

**A WALKER'S TIP**

On fine summer days, when we are tempted into our shorts, it's easy to forget that paths can become overgrown with nettles, so carry a set of waterproof over-trousers to slip on if the nettles are too dense!

takes the footpath to Hagworthingham. Also note the modern stone circle as you cross the top of the fields.

## HAGWORTHINGHAM

What's in a name? 'Hag' means boggy, marshy or rough ground, but Domesday Book has the village called Hacberdingham after Hacberd, a Saxon lord. Over time this has become Hagworth. 'Ing' is said to mean 'people' or 'group' and 'Ham' means homestead, so putting it all together you get Hacberd's-people's-homestead or Hagworth-ing-ham. It is a pleasant village with some lovely cottages, a cafe, pub, a bridged ford and an old manor house. Holy Trinity church with its squat tower, 'ancient and solid' according to Yates and Thorold, was restored in 1859. The tower collapsed in 1972 and the bells had to be sold to repair it.

Our route leaves the village at the ford and enters Furze Hill, a shallow grassy nature reserve with a stream. Look out for opposite-leaved golden-saxifrage by the stream and willow tits amongst the willows and alders. Route finding from here to Mavis Enderby can be difficult when the paths are overgrown but essentially you should follow the stream until overhead power lines cross the path and then bear right.

## MAVIS ENDERBY

St Michael's church was restored in 1878. It is a nice peaceful spot for a breather and looks beautiful, with some gnarled old yews in the churchyard. The yew is an ancient and indigenous tree which was

often planted in churchyards, but many are older than the churches themselves, with some aged over 1,000 years. They have large girths and are often hollow but still growing. The yew is associated with the meeting places of druids and in Christianity it is suggested that the tree's evergreen nature is emblematic of immortality and the Resurrection. The trees are either male or female; the males have yellow flowers which shed clouds of pollen in early spring. The female flowers are small, green and barely noticeable but by mid-September they become swollen, turning a beautiful pinky-red. These are very popular with the birds that unwittingly help to spread the seeds.

## RAITHBY BY SPILSBY

Here we find Holy Trinity church, which dates back to the sixteenth century and has some nice old gravestones. Almost next door to the church you will pass Raithby Hall, dating back to 1776, which has a chapel over its stables in which John Wesley preached.

## HEDGEROWS

From here to Old Bolingbroke, look for common hedgerow-dwelling birds such as the yellowhammer, chaffinch and tree sparrow. The taken-for-granted hedge is a living part of our heritage and something we should be proud of, as regards its natural history value. Most hedges date back to the Enclosure Acts in the eighteenth and nineteenth century. At this time hedges were mainly of single species such as hawthorn and it is this fact which allows us to crudely tell the age of a hedge. The formula is that the older the hedge the greater the variety of shrubs within it (see Kids' Stuff).

We need to be very careful as we have uprooted and destroyed many of our ancient hedges in the name of agricultural progress and we can ill afford to lose any more. As David Robinson points out, 'whilst one would not think about demolishing a Norman castle, second thoughts are seldom given to a hedge of similar age.' Species to look out for are hawthorn, blackthorn, hazel, privet, crab apple, elder, holly, spindle tree, dog rose, and don't forget to count the trees too.

## OLD BOLINGBROKE

Entering Old Bolingbroke, you pass the entrance to Sow Dale, the third of the Wolds dales reserves, with similar fauna and flora to Snipe Dales and

Furze Hill. It is particularly noted for its spotted orchids, marsh marigolds and giant horsetails, looking pretty much as they did in prehistoric times. There is little to let you know how important this place once was and what history lies behind these quiet lanes.

Bolingbroke was described by Yates and Thorold as a 'place of character', which is praise indeed from them. In Domesday Book it had a market, three mills and an annual fair, which indicates that it was already an important place. The name means 'twisty brook of Bulla's people'.

John of Gaunt built the church of St Peter and St Paul from local greenstone. It is richly decorated with a massive solid pinnacled tower and set amongst more yew trees. Some of the 'floriated' medieval stone carving is worth looking at and there are some excellent gargoyles and corbels outside, but once again Yates and Thorold are bemused by the restoration, intimating that it was a nice church 'but James Fowler has been here'! This apart, there is a nice monument and some beautiful lichen-covered gravestones in the churchyard.

The jewel of Old Bolingbroke are the remains of the hexagonal sandstone castle with its corner towers. At one time its walls were 12 feet thick and it was protected by a moat some 30 yards wide. It was the residence of John of Gaunt, the Duke of Lancaster. His son, the future Henry IV, was born here in 1367. The castle was constructed around 1220–30 by Randulph de Blundeville, Earl of Chester after he had returned from the Crusades. John of Gaunt inherited

it through marriage to Blanche of Lancaster, who died of the plague in 1369. Gaunt was also a patron of Geoffrey Chaucer, who would have visited the castle several times.

The castle was damaged by Parliamentarian forces after the Battle of Winceby and the last bits crumbled away and fell down in 1815, leaving just mounds on the ground, the moat and a few bits of masonry. One part of the masonry is the remains of a cellar, which was said to be haunted by a luminous white hare which was, in fact, the spirit of a witch who was once imprisoned here. Apparently the hare would put in appearances at meetings, running between people's legs. They would then chase it with dogs into this escape-proof cellar and, on entering, find nothing but terrified cowering dogs.

Look south-east from the castle towards the high ground and you will see Hall Hill, an ancient burial ground and cremation cemetery. People would bring their dead some distance to these communal grounds.

# Kids' Stuff

## FIND:
**Different types of trees.** This is a great opportunity to get to grips with tree identification so see how many different types you can find on this walk! Before setting off go to www.naturedetectives.org.uk and download leaf, seed and twig identification sheets to take with you. You can also collect some samples to bring home to identify in more detail. This is best done in winter or early spring, before the buds burst into life.

## PLAY:
**Hedge ageing.** Most hedges were once just a single species, but over the years they have been gradually colonised by other shrubs and trees whose seeds are usually transported by the wind and bird droppings. A scientist called Dr Max Hooper devised a surprisingly accurate formula (called Hooper's Law) for dating hedges. He found that one new species established itself every 100 years in any 30-metre stretch. So the age of the hedge is roughly the number of species of tree and shrub in a 30-metre section multiplied by 100. See if you can work out the age of the hedges around you!

## TRY:
**Re-enacting the Civil War.** At Winceby take a look at the lie of the land and try to see the best place where you would position your troops. At Bolingbroke Castle, look out from the walls and decide whether the castle is in a good defensive position or not. Split into two teams. Team 1 has to close their eyes whilst Team 2 hides and takes up a defensive position. Team 1 then have to try to creep up on them without being ambushed. Civil War costumes are optional.

## LOOK UP:
Lichens
Geoffrey Chaucer
Druids

The rituals they undertook here are said to have helped them to strengthen their group identity and sense of community.

## ASGARBY

Here only a churchyard remains after St Swithin's church fell into disuse and was demolished. The overgrown graves, smothered in ivy and brambles, give the place a rather creepy feel. Prehistoric flints have been found here as well as an Anglo-Saxon burial. The route between here and Hameringham is also a particularly good place to spot hares.

## HAMERINGHAM

All Saints church fell down and was entirely restored in 1893. Inside, the thirteenth-century nave survives as well as a medieval font. There is also some good stained glass in the west window.

On the path out of Hammeringham, where the footpath crosses the road at Old Ash, take a look to the north-west and you will see the depression of Slash Hollow, where the Battle of Winceby came to its end with the slaughtering of fleeing Royalist troops. It is said that they came across a gate which opened inwards and so were trapped and at the mercy of the pursuing Parliamentarians.

Further along the path, at its top, there are views of both the wolds and fens and on clear days one can see both Lincoln Cathedral to the east and Boston Stump to the south. We cannot be entirely sure, but as you get close to Winceby the evidence suggests that you may well be walking right over the site of the battle!

*Further Reading*

Robinson, D.N., 'The Lincolnshire Hedge' in *Lincolnshire Life*
www.hedgelink.org.uk/files/a_little_rough_guide_around_the_hedges.pdf
www.battlefieldstrust.com
www.british-trees.com

# TETFORD AND TENNYSON COUNTRY

This route is a 13½-mile figure of eight with Tetford at the centre, where you can park by the church or village hall. The walk is Grade 4 due mainly to length and the occasional hill, but the paths are easy to follow.

## TETFORD

The quiet charm of the Wolds' unhurried and peaceful landscape around Tetford is what sets it apart. It's almost as if it's not tainted by the modern world and is an Area of Outstanding Natural Beauty, with many facets.

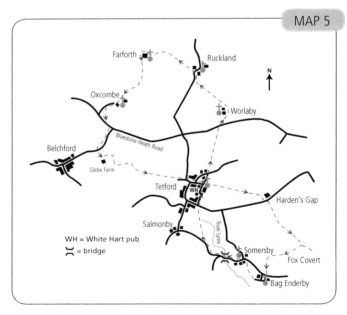

MAP 5

Farforth
Ruckland
N
Oxcombe
Worlaby
Bluestone Heath Road
Belchford
Glebe Farm
Tetford
WH
Harden's Gap
Salmonby
River Lymn
WH = White Hart pub
⊃⊂ = bridge
Somersby
Fox Covert
Bag Enderby

Tetford holds an annual scarecrow festival in early May, which is well worth coinciding the walk with.

Inhabited since prehistoric times, its gently rolling chalk hills contain a wealth of wildlife and hide many tiny villages which have long been the centre of small bustling farming communities. Most walking paths in the Wolds give the walker the opportunity to experience leafy lanes and famous Lincolnshire wide open skies. On a fine summer's day, one can often only see the blue of the sky and below it a bewildering spectrum of different greens. Hedge, tree, field and verge come together to form an endless patchwork quilt of a landscape. This green peace gets shattered by vibrant poppies in late June to leave a stunning combination.

Traditional village pubs offers the thirsty walker some respite and the village churches similarly offer a peaceful welcome. Many farming communities in the Wolds followed the model of a manor house, with a few farmworkers' cottages attached alongside the farm buildings and a chapel. These small chapels are an oasis of quiet solitude and an insight into the area's history. The two we encounter at Farforth and Oxcombe will make you smile to realise that such places still exist. The other major feature of this route is of course its Tennyson connections and these give us a literary opportunity not to be missed, as we are able to make real connections between the poet's words and the landscape which inspired them.

## ST MARY'S CHURCH

Built in 1340, St Mary's church is the first feature we meet on this walk. It has some superb lichen-encrusted gargoyles grimacing down at you as you pass. Outside in the graveyard is a headstone to two gypsies, Tyso Boswell and Edward Hearin, who were killed by the same lightning strike in 1831 and buried together. The mansion house in the village was home to the Dymoke family, who held the title of Champion to the king or queen and used to challenge to single combat anyone denying the monarch's right to succeed at their coronation. Original armour is hung over Captain Edward Dymoke's (champion to George II) memorial in the church.

## WORLABY, RUCKLAND AND FARFORTH

Now follow the road around the back of the church, which swings north, and at a junction after a quarter of a mile, take the footpath straight ahead. This looks as if it is going through somebody's back garden, and indeed it is. Carry on and go through the field taking you to the bottom of the longest hill of the day. Slog up here (if the field is full of waist-high oilseed rape and it's been raining, you might want to put your leggings on) but remember to keep turning around and taking in the view behind you, beyond the village. From the top of the hill, head across the Bluestone Heath Road. This ancient trackway dates back to prehistoric times and clings to the crest of the Wolds for 14 miles.

You then walk through the old farmstead of Worlaby, following the farm road past the old fishponds to Ruckland, where you must visit the first of the small churches to be encountered today. The church of St Olave (or Olaf) is one of the smallest churches in Lincolnshire, seating only forty people and built in 1885. Over the road an elevated track leads you on to Farforth and the church of St Peter, which was rebuilt in 1861 using some medieval fragments. It houses a fifteenth-century font and is a beautiful tranquil place, with a small churchyard which is home to spotted flycatchers in the summer. They can be seen flitting nervously from gravestone to gravestone in their seemingly eternal quest for insects to feed their nearby brood.

It is worth lingering here to look closely at the well-carved gravestones and to just sit inside and admire the beauty. Those who get to worship here can count themselves blessed. Then follow the path here which turns south towards Oxcombe.

## OXCOMBE

This is a remote valley and farmstead tucked away in the middle of the Wolds and generally known to only the few who happen upon it. There is a manor house, farm building and a few cottages, but its highlight is the small All Saints church. There was a church here from the thirteenth century, but the current one was built in 1842 in the perpendicular style. It has a beautiful octagonal tower and upon entering the church you cannot but feel a sense of other worldliness as if you are stepping back in time.

There is an impressive fifteen-century octagonal font and the family pews give you a sense of the social order of the day. Perhaps the most intriguing aspect of the church, though, is the memorials, which have some beautifully worded inscriptions. Thomas Grant died at the age of 46 in 1810, but was suddenly deprived of his 'reason' some years before this. The inscription reads:

Here cooly rests, released from all his earthly woes,
Lull'd by the hand of death, to sweet and calm repose;
The sad remains of one, whose once unsullied mind,
Alike knew how to feel, be generous just and kind;
Till dire disease at length, with awful terror came,
And rudely shook the tablet of his mental frame.

Climb the small road out of Oxcombe and take the first path on the left, which will bring you back out onto the Bluestone Heath Road. Continue left and then right at the junction down the hill towards Belchford. As the road flattens out, take the bridleway on the left towards Glebe Farm Low Yard. This bridleway takes you back into Tetford and completes the first 8-mile section of our figure of eight.

IN LOVING MEMORY OF
ANN
THE BELOVED WIFE OF
WILLIAM BAUMBER OF CADWELL
WHO DIED JAN 3RD 1874
AGED 67 YEARS

AND WHEN THESE FAILING LIPS GROW DUMB,
AND THOUGHT AND MEMORY FLEE,
WHEN THOU SHALT IN THY KINGDOM COME,
THEN LORD, REMEMBER ME.

## THE WHITE HART

The White Hart pub has sixteenth-century origins, low beams and stone flag floors. There is also an old oak settle where Tennyson must surely have sat once, whilst discoursing with his friends and smoking strong shag in a clay pipe, as was his wont. He may well also have played skittles. Samuel Johnson also used to 'sup' here.

Fully refreshed for the next 5½ miles, head back to the church and take a path out of the back of the churchyard which runs almost due east across the fields towards 'Harden's Gap'. This track follows the course of a Roman road to Burgh-le-Marsh, which at the time was a ferry port with vessels crossing the Wash to Norfolk. Go left here and almost immediately right along a bridleway which heads uphill before passing 'Snake Holt' and coming out at a junction at a fox covert. Go right here and this track brings you to the village of Bag Enderby and the beginning of the Tennyson connections.

## BAG ENDERBY

'Bag' derives from the Middle-English word 'Bagge' meaning bag. This describes the topography of the village, with the roads going round in a U shape with the church at the bottom of the bag. 'Ender' comes from the Norse name Eindrithi and 'by' is Danish (for the Vikings were here in numbers) for farmstead or village.

St Margaret's church dates from 1407, built of local Spilsby sandstone. Parliamentarian troops mustering for the Battle of Winceby in 1643 knocked it about a bit, smashing some of the stained-glass windows and the churchyard cross, but it still exists today pretty much as it was. There is a superb limestone font with carvings of the Passion of Christ on each face. Some of these are quite strange, such as a hart licking what appears to be a tree growing out of its back. The church door is never locked and it is a rare oasis of peace and calm.

Nearby is a mud and stud cottage. From here the path takes you across the fields to Somersby, a path Tennyson would have taken many times between the two churches where his father was rector.

### MUD AND STUD COTTAGES

This is the traditional Lincolnshire building method. Studs are upright wooden posts between which is stuck a mixture of mud, straw, cow dung, horse hair and lime to form a wall. This is then whitewashed and traditionally topped off with a thatched roof.

## SOMERSBY

St Margaret's church and the rectory are the focus here. The church was built in the fifteenth century using greenstone, the local iron-rich sandstone. Tennyson was baptised in the font and in the churchyard lies the tomb of his father. The church has a Tennyson exhibition and a bust of the bard. Over the road, next to the castellated brick house and hiding behind some topiary, is the rectory where Tennyson was born and lived until the age of 28.

From Somersby, head west along the road, passing over the tiny River Lymn. Follow this road for about a mile as it twists and turns, until you come to a bridleway on the left which will take you back into Tetford for another well-earned pint.

## TENNYSON

The Poet Laureate Alfred Lord Tennyson was born at the rectory in Somersby on 6 August 1809. His father was the rector here and the landscape of his early years is enshrined in his poetry. Flowing through the village is the River Lymn which is the subject of his poem 'The Brook':

I come from haunts of coot and hern,
I make a sudden sally
And sparkle out among the fern,
To bicker down a valley.

I chatter over stony ways,
In little sharps and trebles,
I bubble into eddying bays,
I babble on the pebbles

For men may come and men may go
But I go on forever.

The church at Somersby and the neighbouring church across the fields at Bag Enderby have small Tennyson exhibitions. Tennyson began writing poetry from an early age. At the age of 7 his father sent him to Louth's grammar school, where he spent four unhappy years suffering from bullying and severe discipline. After this he returned to the rectory at Somersby and was taught by his father. The home would have been very crowded, with six brothers and four sisters, along with the servants and various pets. Tennyson was a bit of a free spirit, wandering around the lanes and fields at all hours, book in hand.

Tennyson Land.

The Brook and Bridge.

Somersby.

The Woodman's Cottage.
"I wind about, and in and out,
With here a blossom sailing,
And here and there a lusty trout,
And here and there a grayling."

## A Life of Tragedy

His father, George Clayton Tennyson, suffered terribly from depression and epilepsy and became dependent on drink and opium. He was unpredictable, flew into violent rages and had long bouts of despair. Thus this was a very unhappy time for the young Tennyson and he took solace in his writing, going to Cambridge University in 1827. There he became lifelong friends with Arthur Hallam, who later became engaged to his sister Emily (Tennyson was to later call his son Hallam). Tennyson remained at Cambridge until his father died in 1831, whereupon he returned to Somersby to take charge of the household. Tragically, his friend Arthur died of a stroke in Venice aged just 22 and this had a huge impact upon Tennyson, who buried his own grief in order to support his sister Emily. In 1837, with two brothers suffering from mental health problems, the family moved to Epping Forest, but financial problems dogged Tennyson.

## Better Times

At the age of 41, 1850 was to be a good year for Tennyson. He had written many poems whilst grieving for the loss of Arthur and an anonymous (he was sensitive to criticism) volume called *In Memoriam A.H.H* was published. It was a great success, giving him financial security, and was said to have given great comfort to Queen Victoria after Prince Albert's death in 1861. The volume also brought him back in touch with his boyhood sweetheart Emily Sellwood (a relative of the Lincolnshire explorer John Franklin of Spilsby). That same year they married and the Poet Laureate William Wordsworth died, with Tennyson becoming his successor. By 1853, Tennyson and Emily had established a home on the Isle of Wight where they became friends with photographer Julia Margaret Cameron and artist George Frederick Watts. In the early 1890s he was earning £10,000 a year, an immense sum then, but also an indication of his popularity. Tennyson died in 1892 and is buried in Westminster Abbey, but there is a fitting local tribute of a large bronze sculpture of Tennyson and his faithful wolfhound by his friend G.F. Watts in the grounds of Lincoln Cathedral.

## WILDLIFE

Farming has long been the lifeblood of this region and, in essence, little has changed over the years. The fields have grown a little larger and a few hedges have disappeared, but on the whole the area retains a sense of yesterday and comfortingly feels quite out of touch with the rest of the world. Lincoln Red cattle eye you lazily as you saunter past and typical Lincolnshire wildlife abounds, with hares and foxes sneaking along the lanes and field edges. Barn owls hunt the same lanes at dawn and dusk and yellowhammers sing from the hedge tops at the height of the day. With their bright yellow heads they are the nearest we have to a British canary. They have a large bill and are mainly seedeaters, forming flocks in winter with other finches which flit over the stubble fields in search of grain. They are a typical Lincolnshire farm bird, but one that is declining with the destruction of hedgerows. You are most likely to notice the bird in spring and summer, when the male sits atop a hedge singing its song which sounds like he's saying 'a little bit of bread and no cheese'.

# Kids' Stuff

**WRITE:**
**A poem.** Write a poem about this walk and the scenery you encounter.

**PLAY:**
**Bird watching.** This is too good a walk not to try and get a good list of birds spotted to be the best twitcher. Prizes for spotting a kingfisher and green woodpecker.

**FIND:**
**Skylarks.** The whole of the route is excellent for skylark-spotting competitions. You will often hear them overhead but who will spot them first?

**Foxes.** Foxes are often seen along this route, especially early in the morning, so keep an eye out.

**DRAW:**
**Gargoyle.** Sketch those you see on the walk and then try and invent your own which are scarier and weirder.

**LOOK UP:**
Gargoyle
Tennyson
Wold
Lincolnshire Red

The many flocks of rooks are never long out of earshot either, whilst their cousins, the jackdaws, typically hang around the church towers. Spotted flycatchers can also be seen flitting about chasing insects in one or two churchyards in the summer, so take the opportunity to sit quietly and just watch for a while. Tennyson's brook also harbours a secret guest; it is home to freshwater crayfish, a species that indicates clean water. Butterflies, bees and bugs also abound and in summer, when trees like limes are in flower, you can hear them as you approach, buzzing and humming! Stop and look up into them and you can see the manic activity of thousands of different insects going about their business.

## LINCOLNSHIRE WEATHER AND DIALECT

This walk is an opportunity to experience Lincolnshire weather and practice some Lincolnshire dialect. Should you encounter rain you will have to decide whether it is 'siling', ''kelching', 'teaming', 'puthering', 'jugging' or merely 'mizzling' down! If this is so, you will need to 'yerk' up your trousers. This refers to tying the trouser legs with a piece of twine to hold them off the floor and stop them getting wet. It is also useful for stopping mice running up your legs at harvest time, or when clearing out the barn. Later in the year, when it is not very warm, then it must be 'cowd' as it often is towards 'back end' (Autumn). At this time of year the weather is often best described as 'owery' i.e; overcast, damp, cold and drizzly. And in winter it can often be 'snide' when the wind is especially cold and cuts right through you and the roads and paths might well be 'slaape' (slippery). But that's enough 'chittering' for now.

The overwhelming memory you will take away from this beautiful spot is that of peace, quiet, charm and a sense of unhurriedness, where in this 'haunt of ancient peace' Tennyson's lark can 'scarce get out his notes for joy'.

_Further Reading_

Robinson, D.N. (ed.), _The Lincolnshire Wolds_, (Oxbow Books; Oxford, 2009)
Tennyson, A., 'The Gardener's Daughter', 'Maud' and 'The Brook' in _The Poetical Works of Alfred Lord Tennyson, Poet Laureate_ (MacMillan & Co. Ltd; London, 1899)
www.lincswolds.org.uk
www.lincolnshirewolds.info

# BETWEEN TWO MARKETS

Spilsby to Alford

MAP 6

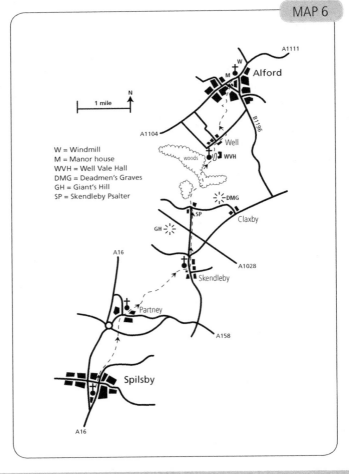

W = Windmill
M = Manor house
WVH = Well Vale Hall
DMG = Deadmen's Graves
GH = Giant's Hill
SP = Skendleby Psalter

This 8-mile walk links two historic market towns and explores many different aspects of Lincolnshire's heritage. Alford Manor House Museum makes a fitting finale to this walk, as it brings back to life some of the lost heritage. Also to be explored en route are the tiny hamlet of Well (with its hall, parkland and church), the village of Partney and, in Spilsby, the story of Sir John Franklin, the Arctic explorer who was born there in 1786. The walk is a Grade 2, with good paths for the bulk of the walk and straightforward navigation.

## SPILSBY

The name Spilsby is said to derive from a Dane called 'Spillir' who owned a 'by', or small settlement, hereabouts. Market day in Spilsby has been a Monday since it was awarded its charter over 700 years ago in 1302. Here until the eighteenth century, according to Marsden, you could buy and sell a wife for 10 shillings. Market stalls were set up under the five arches of what used to be the old town hall, gaol and court. In the east market

place there is a fourteenth-century medieval Buttercross, whose steps would have been used for both selling and preaching. There is also a bronze memorial statue to Sir John Franklin, Spilsby's most famous son.

Whilst Spilsby was a relatively small market town, it was still a stopping point on the coach service from Louth to London in the eighteenth century and the White Hart, once thatched, was the major coaching inn.

St James' church has a pinnacled tower and is strangely restored, with only its tower still displaying the traditional Spilsby greenstone and the rest having been covered with Ancaster stone in 1879. Many of the churches you will see in the Wolds are made from what is called 'Spilsby Sandstone', also called greenstone because of its blueish-green hue caused by the presence of the mineral glauconite. As it ages, this weathers to an attractive warm and rusty colour. This rock was laid down 140 million years ago when it was the bed of a shallow sea.

In the early 1300s the 'manor' of Spilsby passed to Robert Willoughby de Eresby, whose family dominated the town until the nineteenth century. The church is similarly dominated, with the Willoughby Chapel containing some

You can have a good weekend by combining the walk with the annual Spilsby Show.

of the finest medieval tombs in the country. The Willoughbys have seven tombs in all, dating from 1349 to 1610. Some are recumbent alabaster figures in armour with their wives and one, John, even has his legs crossed.

The church also has a memorial tablet to Sir John Franklin which simply states of their North West Passage discovery, 'They forged the last link with their lives'.

## FRANKLIN

Sir John Franklin was born here in 1786 in a bakery in the high street, which has a plaque to this effect. He joined the navy at 14 and undertook a circumnavigation of Australia in 1801–3. He also fought the French at Trafalgar under Nelson whilst still a teenager and later developed an interest in finding a north-west passage to the Indies via the Arctic coast of Canada. He commanded an overland mapping expedition there in 1819 and when food ran out his men resorted to eating lichens and animal carcasses they found, and chewing boot leather. At the age of 59 he sailed there again with two ships, *Erebus* and *Terror*. They were last seen that July. In 1859 a cairn and his logbook were found, showing that they had discovered the passage but then had to abandon their ships as they became ice locked. Franklin's body was never discovered. On his memorial in Westminster Abbey his nephew, Tennyson, described him as a 'heroic sailor soul'.

Spilsby's other claim to fame is that in 1765 Thomas Paine was posted as excise officer here, as the area was notorious for smuggling. After a year he emigrated to America, where he wrote the book *The Rights of Man* and helped to write the Declaration of Independence.

## PARTNEY

Take care crossing the A158 Partney bypass on the way into the village. There used to be a Saxon monastery here but it has disappeared without trace. Likewise, there used to be three annual sheep fairs but this has been replaced with an annual fete. The church of St Nicholas has a high nave and tall tower and is set amongst yew trees. The capitals of the pillars are heavily carved with foliage and there are a large number of grotesquely carved heads around the arches. Outside in the graveyard there is a stone commemorating the marriage of Matthew Flinders, the explorer and cousin of Sir John Franklin.

## SKENDLEBY

St Peter and St Paul church is heavily restored but it is a fine sight as you tramp across the fields from Partney. It is early English and has a medieval font and some nice modern stained glass. From the churchyard there are fine views of the Grade II listed Skendleby Hall which dates back to the mid-1700s and is an interesting mix of architectural styles, being part Georgian, Elizabethan and Victorian with an unusual clock tower and its own chapel. Also worthy of note is the Blacksmiths Arms, once the village smithy and now a good excuse for a breather.

## NEOLITHIC AND CRETACEOUS LANDSCAPE

Climbing out of Skendleby, but out of sight to the west, is the site of Giant's Hill, a long barrow dating back to 3500 BC. Underneath the unimpressive low mound is a pair of Neolithic burial chambers and archaeologists claim that at least eight burials have taken place there. A little further on, as we drop down into the hamlet of Skendleby Psalter about a mile to the east, and again unsighted, lie the better-preserved burial chambers called Deadmen's Graves, dated at around 4000 BC. These people were the earliest farmers who worked the lower ground, keeping sheep, goats, pigs and cattle, and the chambers would have been communal graves. Between Skendleby and Skendleby Psalter look out for the arable weed scarlet pimpernel with its tiny star-shaped red flowers.

The underlying rock hereabouts is chalk, laid down as the seabed in the Cretaceous period (around 140–75 million years ago) The chalk is made up of the shells of billions of marine creatures, such as the bivalve mollusc *Inoceramus*. This chalk has long been put to use supplying stone for roads across the local marshes and lime for fertiliser. The chalk also brings with it a flora rich in calcium-loving plants, such as salad burnet, bell flower and cowslips, and this walk is a good one for testing your identification skills.

## WELL

As you approach Well you emerge from woodland into parkland and catch sight of Well Vale Hall. As you near it you pass the superb isolated Georgian church, built to resemble a Greek temple with a pediment and cupola supported by four Tuscan columns. There are views across the lake of the red-brick Georgian Well Vale Hall, built by James Bateman in 1725. Yates and Thorold call it 'the most beautiful setting of any house in Lincolnshire'. The lake is fed by a chalk spring and this keeps it exceptionally clear and welcoming to wildlife. Note too the wonderful beech and oak trees as you pass the hall. The walk from here takes us back across farmland into Alford and at harvest time there is the reminder that our farming heritage is constantly moving on with ever more modern machinery.

## ALFORD

You could not wish for a finer example of a typical Lincolnshire market town to end the walk with. Alford's name derives from a stream crossing here, where long ago people would have gathered to buy and sell their wares such as Wolds wool, barley, meat, fish and salt from the coastal villages. The Lincoln Red Bull Fair also used to be held in Alford every year. These handsome shorthorn cattle are thought to derive originally from Viking stock. The deep cherry-red coats make them instantly recognisable and they are a handsome feature of the Lincolnshire landscape.

The church of St Wilfred was built upon an artificial mound around 1350 but was 'over restored' in 1869. One of Alford's strongly puritan vicars, the Rev. Francis Marbury, was also the headmaster of the grammar school. He had

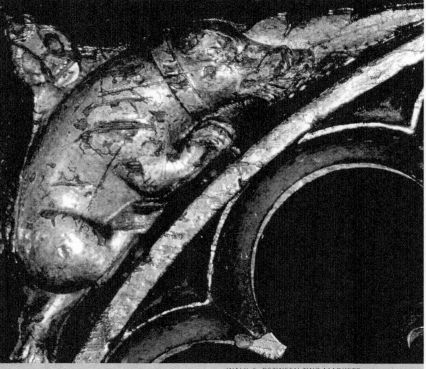

a daughter, Anne, who was one of the earliest campaigners for free speech. She married William Hutchinson, one of the Pilgrim Fathers, and emigrated to Boston, Massachusetts where she became America's first female preacher. After the death of her husband and falling out with the established puritans, she moved to a remote area of Long Island where, along with five of her children, she was killed by Native Americans in 1643.

The Rev. Marbury also taught Captain John Smith, who went to school here in the 1590s. Captain Smith was captured by Native Americans whilst exploring but was saved from execution by the 12-year-old Pocahontas. Inside the church, note the fruit and flower carvings on the capitals of the slender pillars and the ornately carved Jacobean pulpit. In one corner of the screen is a carving of a small dog, so see if you can spot him. Religion played a strong role locally and one street is called 'Ranters Row' named after the Primitive Methodist preachers who were nicknamed 'Ranters' because of their lively sermons and services.

There is also an ornate monument to Sir Robert Christopher and his wife. Christopher built the seventeenth-century, thatched, brick manor house in 1611. This is now a folk museum and tea rooms. The adjoining Hackett Barn Museum houses many of Alford's historic artefacts and reminders of Lincolnshire's farming heritage. There is also a bootmakers and an outside wooden lavatory!

The town was ravaged by the plague in 1630 when 131 people died out of a population of less than 500. Food and supplies were left outside the town, where a large hollowed-out stone full of vinegar was used to disinfect money given in exchange.

The year 1884 saw the opening of the Alford and Sutton Steam Tramway, which ran on a 2-foot 6-inch gauge track through the town to the coast 7 miles away at Sutton-on-Sea. It was to be superseded two years later in 1886 by the coming of the railways. Heading north from the church will bring you to the five-sailed Alford Mill, built in 1813. It could reputedly grind 5 tons of corn a day and stands at 95 feet with six floors. The art of the miller well and truly lives on here, and in its heyday the town also had several other mills.

*Further Reading*

Marsden, W., *Lincolnshire* (Batsford; London, 1977)
Martineau, H.D., 'A Cameo of Alford' in *Lincolnshire Life* (Dec 1967)
Yates, J. and H. Thorold, *Lincolnshire: A Shell Guide* (Faber and Faber; London, 1965)

# Kids' Stuff

**WATCH:**
**Pocahontas.** This Disney cartoon does stay true to some of the facts, but it also adjusts them to try to make a better story. Check out the real story online after you have watched it and decide if you think the truth has been distorted too much! In relation to other matters Disney, I am sorry to have to tell you that Robin Hood was not a fox!

**FIND:**
**A scarlet pimpernel.** This tiny red star-shaped flower is a common weed of farmland and flowers in July and August. First to spot one wins a prize.
**A bell flower.** Somewhat easier to see, but just as good a find is the large bell flower which likes calcium-rich chalky soil.
**A bull.** But don't get too close!

**MAKE:**
**Some bread.** Whilst at the mill buy a bag of flour and when you get home make a loaf of bread or some buns. It tastes so much better when you have made it yourself.

**TRY:**
**Your wildflower identification skills.** Take a good field guide with you and try and identify all the flowers you come across which you don't know the names of. If you are still not sure, take a photo and try and identify it back at home.

**FIND OUT:**
**How a windmill works.** Just what are all those cogs for and how does it grind the corn? Take a look at www.wikipedia.org/wiki/mill_machinery.

**LOOK UP:**
Inoceramus
Wodwose

# LOUTH

## The Navigation Canal and Tetney Marshes

This consists of three walks (6, 9 and 12 miles) centred around the Louth Navigation Canal. The first route out and back from Louth (6 miles) follows the canal to Alvingham with its mill and twin churches. At the other end of the canal there is a circuit of 9 miles which takes in Tetney lock, the 'blow wells' and Tetney Marshes Nature Reserve. The full 12-mile route follows the canal from Louth to its outflow at Tetney Marshes. It is a Grade 4

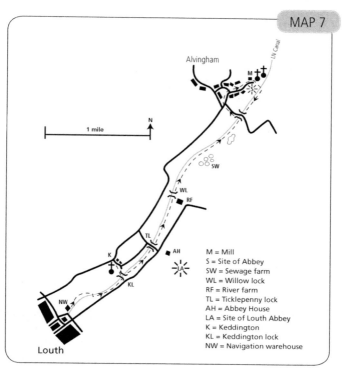

MAP 7

Alvingham

LN Canal

1 mile    N

M = Mill
S = Site of Abbey
SW = Sewage farm
WL = Willow lock
RF = River farm
TL = Ticklepenny lock
AH = Abbey House
LA = Site of Louth Abbey
K = Keddington
KL = Keddington lock
NW = Navigation warehouse

Louth

because, despite its length, the going is easy and navigation simple. There is parking at the start of the canal in Louth and in Alvingham, Tetney lock and on the roadside by the church near the reserve at Tetney Blow Wells.

## LOUTH TO ALVINGHAM

The canal starts life at the Riverhead area of Louth, which was at the heart of the bustling canal trade. Navigation warehouse, an old 1770s wool warehouse, stands proud here. The 12-mile-long canal was built to carry grain and wool out to the Humber ports of Grimsby and Hull and to bring back coal for domestic heating and timber for building. It took nearly seven years to build the canal with its eight locks and it would have been a fine sight in its heyday, with barges plying to and fro. Some of the locks were specially built to a barrel-shaped design in order to withstand the pressure from the surrounding farmland and marshes. These can be best seen at the Ticklepenny and Willows locks.

Ticklepenny lock was named after the Ticklepenny family who were local farmers and lock-keepers. Members of the family are buried in St Margaret's church, Keddington, just a short walk across the fields. This is well worth the short diversion and the Ticklepenny graves are on the left of the church path just after the porch. Also, just before the porch, look at the small Saxon window with the strange creature carved above it. This is commonly thought to be a seal. We are not sure why this is, but then we are only a few miles from Donna Nook, which from November is home to one of the largest grey seal colonies in the UK.

The canal now follows the River Lud to Alvingham where, by the footbridge, which we cross, you can see one of the original canal milestones. Kingfishers are frequently seen along this stretch. Alvingham's main claim to fame is in having two churches in one churchyard. St Adelwold's is the parish church for Alvingham, whilst St Mary's is the parish church for North Cockerington. St Adelwold was a bishop on the island of Lindisfarne and this is the only church in the country dedicated to him. St Mary's (now redundant) has box pews, is a Grade I listed building and lies about half a mile from its parish of Cockerington on the other side of the canal. Look out for the grave of James Lucas which bears the inscription, 'Remember me as you pass by, As you are now so once was I: As I am now so must you be, Prepare yourself to follow me.' Other inscriptions are equally interesting. Look out too for Alice, the wife of John Taylor.

St Mary's was originally the chapel for the Gilbertine priory here, but after the Dissolution of the Monasteries it was given to North Cockerington because their church was in such a bad state of repair. It dates from the eleventh century, with the tower being added in the nineteenth. It also

has a thirteenth-century font and fragments of a stone coffin bearing the effigy of a knight with a lion at his feet. In the nearby fields you can just see the traces of the Gilbertine priory. The Gilbertine order was founded by St Gilbert in 1130 in Lincolnshire. It is said that Edward I (or Edward Longshanks, as he was known because he was 6 feet 2 inches tall) sent Gwenllian, the daughter of Llywelyn II, here after his defeat of the Welsh in 1282. She was subsequently sent to the priory at Sempringham where she remained for the rest of her life. The Alvingham priory was active until most of its inhabitants died from the Black Death. Just past the church through the farmyard is Alvingham Mill, an old seventeeth-century watermill (now a private residence).

The short walk now retraces its steps back to Louth. Looking to the left at Ticklepenny lock is Abbey House, behind which lies the site of the Cistercian Louth Abbey, founded in 1139. It was the dissolution of this abbey which sparked the Lincolnshire Uprising of 1536.

## THE LOUTH NAVIGATION CANAL:
## A HANDMADE WONDER FROM END TO END

The route from Alvingham needs little description as it follows the canal side all the way to Tetney Haven and the marshes. Construction on the canal began in 1765, during the Industrial Revolution, in an attempt to stave off Louth's decline. A great deal of the town's Georgian wealth came from the canal. Work began at the Tetney lock end and the canal didn't reach Louth until 1770. In this part of Lincolnshire at this time, few people travelled more than a few miles from their birth place and there were those who never left their village. The few roads in and out of town were rudimentary and there was not much industry here, but there was a need to export the huge quantities of grain and wool produced by the agricultural economy. The Louth Corporation turned its attention to the new trend for canal building in a desire to make Louth an inland port. The canal was built wide in order to take sloops and keels, which were twice as wide as other canal boats. These vessels could use the canal once a month, only at the highest tides, and were built to be seaworthy enough to stand the often choppy seas at the mouth of the Humber. It took seven years to complete in all and was dug largely by hand with shovels, wheelbarrows and much-sweated labour. The timber for the lock gates was hand sawn, the ironmongery forged locally and the bricks handmade in local village brickyards. The final cost was around £28,000 and the first vessel sailed its full length in 1770. Before long, many granaries, timber yards, boatyards and tanneries were thriving in the Riverhead area. It was also said that at that time (1780-90s), more

# Kids' Stuff

**PLAY:**

**Walking Bingo.** Design a bingo card (4x4) and on it have church, canal, lock, rabbit, kingfisher, fish, weather vane, Lincolnshire Red cow, canal side grainstore, watermill, marestail, oil storage tank, anchor, fisherman, feather and milestone. Prizes for all corners, a line and a full house.

**Bird racing.** The first to get twenty species wins the prize.

**DRAW:**

**A canalscape.** This is a challenge, but the trick is to carefully study the horizon and see what features you can add to make it interesting, such as church towers. Try putting things right in the foreground in order to give it perspective.

**MAKE:**

**A trail stick.** This is a recommended make for every walk. Northern Native Americans used to keep a record of their journeys by collecting bits of 'stuff' as they went along the way. They could then tell other tribe members how to make the trip by showing them the trail stick. Take a supply of rubber bands with you. First find a stick and each time you find something interesting attach it to the stick with a rubber band. Good things are grasses, feathers, flowers, sprigs of berries, dead rabbits (parental advisory), that sort of thing.

**LOOK UP:**

Artesian springs
Daubenton's bat
Echolocation
Gilbertine
Longshanks
The Black Death
Waterspout
Louth flood of 1920

MAP 8

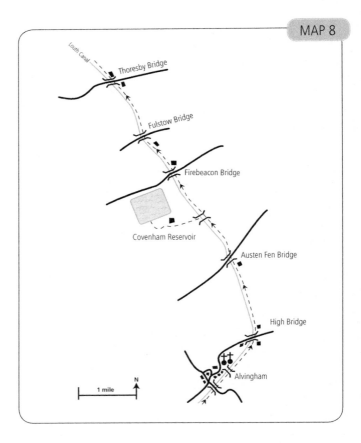

fish was landed at Louth fishmarket than at Grimsby, whose docks had become silted up.

In 1847 the canal came under the control of the railways, whose dominance and advantages were too many for the canal to compete with but it was not until 1924 that the last barge passed down the canal. However, the canal's days were naturally numbered, with its demise partly due to the continual silting up of its outfall at Tetney Haven between the last lock and the sea. The Riverhead area was also damaged by the Louth flood of 1920, said to have been caused by a waterspout and thunderstorms. This unprecedented rainfall on the Wolds west of Louth drained into the River Lud and caused an 'avalanche of water' to surge through the town.

Because the land between Alvingham and Tetney is so flat, no locks were required between Tetney Haven and Outfen lock. There are two eighteenth-century canal-side grain warehouses at Austen Fen and Firebeacon Bridge.

The main features of interest beyond Outfen lock are the tranquillity and wildlife. It is a place to saunter along in peace, spotting herons and mute swans. Look out for kingfishers and little grebes and, in summer, common terns, sedge warblers and yellow wagtails. Keep an eye out for water voles.

Midway between Austen Fen and Firebeacon Bridges is a footbridge over the canal and from here a footpath leads to Covenham Reservoir, which is particularly good for birdwatching. In winter it holds large numbers of wildfowl, including gooseander and goldeneye, as well as sea ducks, grebes and divers.

## TETNEY BLOW WELLS AND MARSHES

You can begin this walk at several points but I prefer to begin at Tetney Blow Wells Park in Church Lane and take the public footpath half a mile past the church which heads south of Tetney Blow Wells. This Lincolnshire Wildlife Trust Reserve consists of a series of blow wells, wet woodland, meadows and old watercress beds. The wells are artesian springs, the exit holes where water under pressure from rainfall on the Wolds escapes

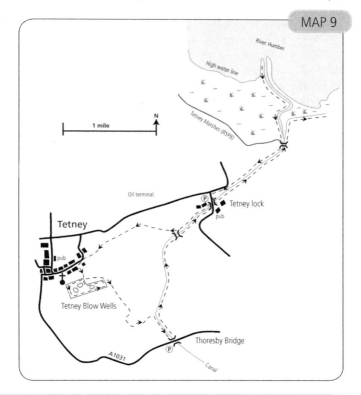

MAP 9

through the underlying chalk and clay to the surface. You can clearly see the old concrete water channels from when these were commercial watercress beds in the 1950s.

This is an excellent reserve for water birds and studying water plants such as water starwort, marestail, great willowherb, water violet and marsh orchid. There are three kinds of bat including the rare Daubenton's bat. This is a fascinating animal; it hibernates for six months and roosts in hollow trees close to water. At dusk they come out to hunt for insects, which they scoop up with their membranous tails and feet. If you're lucky you can see them skimming the water's surface using echolocation to catch their prey. Watch out too for water voles and otters.

The walk from the blow wells heads south-east and dog-legs to Thoresby Bridge where we cross to the other side and join the Louth Navigation Canal on its final leg to the North Sea. Walking along the canal, keeping an eye out for kingfishers, you eventually come to Tetney lock. The Crown and Anchor, dating from the eighteenth century, is a welcome sight here and this area is a haven for fishing. The road bridge replaces the old sea lock and from here it is 10 miles back to Louth along the canal. You may be tempted to call it a draw here and return to the start, but it would be remiss to have come this far and not follow the canal towards its outfall in the sea amidst Tetney Marshes. Walk out along the right-hand bank of the canal for about a mile until you reach a bridge, then follow the sea wall as far as you like, admiring the wilderness this area provides.

Tetney Marshes are an RSPB reserve of coastal mudflats, salt marsh, dunes and saline lagoons. It is an important site for estuary birds in the UK, with at least 175,000 birds using the estuary during the winter months including knot, sanderling, brent geese and grey and golden plover. Twites and hen harriers also winter on the saltmarsh.

The route back follows the canal on its other bank into Tetney lock and then along a track to Tetney village, with the Tetney oil storage terminal shadowing you all the way. Just beside these is the site of a Marconi Beam Station, where telegrams were sent to Australia and India by the Imperial Wireless Chain in the 1920s. In its day it was the most advanced long-distance communication system. Back in the village it is worth a quick visit to the church of St Peter and St Paul, dating from 1363.

--------------------------------------------------------------- *Further Reading*

www.bbc.co.uk/nature/life

www.louthcanal.org.uk

Naylor, E., 'The Louth Navigation Canal' in *Lincolnshire Life* (Dec 1966, Vol. 6, No. 10) pp.42–45

# A TASTE OF
# THE VIKING WAY

## From Caistor to Tealby

MAP 10

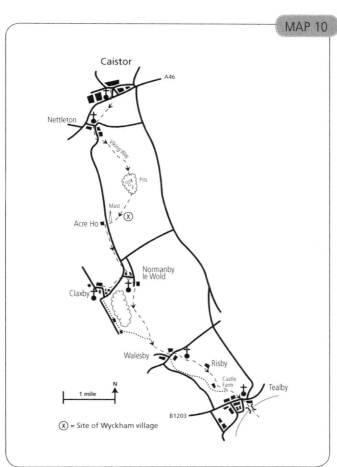

This 12-mile walk takes us out of the typical Lincolnshire market town of Caistor along what could be described as 'The Viking Way's best bits'. It takes in excellent Wolds scenery, fascinating villages and the famous 'Rambler's church' near Walesby, not to mention the highest point in the county. The walk ends at Tealby, often cited as Lincolnshire's prettiest village, and which has Tennyson connections. The best way to do this is to park in Tealby carpark and take a pre-arranged taxi to Caistor (or vice versa). You can also walk a figure of eight or two short loops from Walesby to break the long haul into more manageable proportions. Quite hilly in parts, the long walk achieves a Grade 4, but as it hugs the Viking Way it is well signposted.

## CAISTOR

Before hitting the Viking Way it is well worth spending an hour exploring Caistor. Several springs arise here where the chalk meets boulder clay, ensuring that there has been habitation in this spot for over 2,000 years. The town grew up as a Roman military outpost or camp and developed into a fully fledged Roman walled town, largely due to the fact that it had a good defensive position atop the Wolds, springs and a local source of iron ore. In medieval times the town suffered from the plague and in 1681 it suffered again as fire destroyed all the timber-framed buildings. Most of the current town dates from this point onwards.

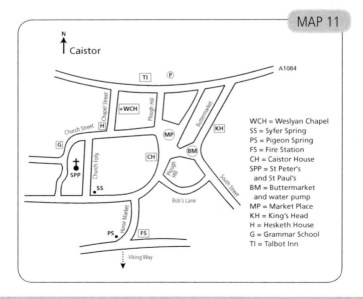

MAP 11

WCH = Weslyan Chapel
SS = Syfer Spring
PS = Pigeon Spring
FS = Fire Station
CH = Caistor House
SPP = St Peter's
    and St Paul's
BM = Buttermarket
    and water pump
MP = Market Place
KH = King's Head
H = Hesketh House
G = Grammar School
TI = Talbot Inn

Beginning in the typical Lincolnshire market square, notice the surrounding Georgian buildings and the town water pump dating from 1897 and commemorating the Diamond Jubilee of Queen Victoria. Caistor House, built in 1682, stands out with its white stucco walls. Note the coats of arms of the Wickham and Walpole families. The house was at one time home to members of the Tennyson family. The Kings Head wine bar built in 1710 was originally a beer house. In the butter market, notice the war memorial, sessions house and White Hart. This is one of only four pubs left; at one time there were twenty-nine! Note the large arches of former inns to allow coaches into the yards. Barley described butter markets as a place for 'women to sit and gossip', whereas the ploughman 'needed the whole square to be sure of meeting all his friends and the pavement was his club'.

From here walk down the picturesque Bob's Lane into Plough Hill. Look down Horsemarket to the tunnel in the hillside with red double doors; this used to house the town's horse-drawn fire engine. By the side of the old fire station is one of the town's springs, known as 'Pigeon Spring'. Turn into Fountain Street and at the bottom you will find another spring called 'Syfer Spring' which used to supply the old brewery across the road.

Next, walk up Church Folly and into the churchyard of St Peter and St Paul. This is built of sandstone and has a buttressed tower with a Norman base. The interior has tall nave arcades and three fourteenth-century effigies, the tombs of two knights, one a crusader and the other Sheriff of Lincoln, and a lady. The south door is impressive and contains thirteenth-century ironwork. Note too, the magnificent Victorian stained glass and the unusual rood beam.

The church also houses the curious 13-foot long 'Gad whip'! This was part of the Palm Sunday ritual whereby a ploughman's whip was taken by a tenant from nearby Broughton to the church. The whip had a purse attached with thirty silver coins in it. It would be cracked three times, first in the porch and then over the clergyman's head during the lessons. It was then placed in the pew of the Lord of Hundon Manor. One legend has it that long ago a boy was beaten to death with a branch of Wych Elm by the lord of the manor for trespassing. Others suggest the ceremony has religious significance linked to St Peter and Judas Iscariot, the money representing Iscariot's payment for betraying Christ. The ceremony was last performed in 1846. Outside the church, hidden in foliage, are some remains of the Roman wall.

Along Church Street you find the old grammar school. Founded in 1631, the stone on the front is inscribed with words from Homer's *Iliad* meaning 'always to excel', the school's motto. Be careful here to check the railings of Hesketh House, as on the corner on of the railings is reputed to be a sword used in the 1536 Lincolnshire Uprising!

Turn into Chapel Street and look at the large Wesleyan Methodist church of 1842 and police house of 1855. Now, turning into High Street, you are on part of the Roman road linking Caistor to Horncastle. The Talbot Inn stands where Caistor's earliest recorded inn stood in 1642.

Take care leaving Caistor as you cross the A46 towards Nettleton.

## NETTLETON

Named in Domesday Book as 'Neteltone' which means 'farmstead where nettles grow'. The church of St John the Baptist, rebuilt in 1874, has a Saxon doorway and the church clock was made in 1837 by the son of James Harrison, whose brother was John Harrison of 'longitude' fame, who made marine chronometers. The nineteenth-century Salutation Inn stands at a busy crossroads and was once an important coaching inn.

A mile or so out of Nettleton, along the beck as you enter some woodland, you will meet evidence of industry. The local area has been mined for iron down the centuries up until 1968. All around this area are bricked-up tunnel entrances to what were ironstone mines. These old tunnels make good bat roosts and Pipistrelles in particular can be seen in good numbers in early evening. The ironstone beds are around 135 million years old and the more recent mining industry revived in 1929 and supplied the steel works at Scunthorpe. The area is rich in interest for the geologist; it gives us a glimpse of the birth of Lincolnshire. Notice the many small valleys gouged out in the Ice Age. These reveal fossil remains which suggest that at one time this was an ancient sea and these ridges possibly islands.

Further along, at the head of Nettleton Valley, is some lumpy ground which indicates the site of a medieval village called Wykeham, which was abandoned, probably due to the plague.

From the chalk Wolds between Nettleton and Normanby, looking west you can see Lincolnshire's limestone ridge with Lincoln Cathedral perched on top some 20 miles away, as the crow flies. Just east of where you now stand, the chalk ridge of the Wolds reaches its highest point at 551 feet, or as the trig point has it, 168 metres above sea level. The Lincolnshire Wolds are in fact the highest ground between Yorkshire and Kent.

## NORMANBY LE WOLD

The name Normanby means 'Norsemen's village' with 'le Wold' being a fairly recent addition. St Peter's church, built of local ironstone, dates from the thirteenth century but was restored in 1868. It has a sixteenth-century gravestone in the south aisle and ten fine oval eighteenth-century German painted glass panels. It also has a strange 'trumpet curl' corbel and a wonderful 'toothache' corbel!

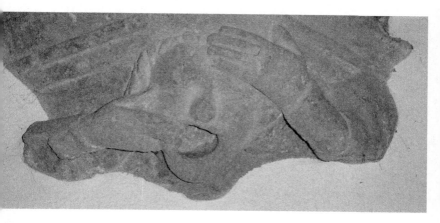

## CLAXBY

When ironstone was discovered in 1859/60, the locals here had high expectations of wealth and expansion, which unfortunately for them were never realised. Fortunately for us however, Russell and Holmes have recorded the village history in fine detail. It is rare to find such a well-researched document and gives us a glimpse of what life was like here in times past. Set at the foot of the Wolds, the thirteenth-century St Mary's church is Early English and was restored and all but rebuilt in 1871.

It has some fine stained glass and a thirteenth-century decorated stone, a 'mutilated' monument, some brasses and a painted nave wall. Take care especially to notice the modern window dedicated to George Ogg, a postman. Be sure to notice his car, an envelope, his gardening tools, the church and his favourite flowers, lily of the valley. Just past the wooden screen, look out for the two stone heads pulling ungodly faces.

Outside, mine workers from Nettleton ironstone pits are buried in the churchyard. It was dangerous work. See if you can find the grave of William Keal, who was only 26 when he died in a mining accident. There are also gravestones for eleven members of the Marshal family and also worthy of note is the sad monument to the Bristow daughters. And finally there is Thomas Brooks, the oldest existing grave in the cemetery. Notice the beautiful lichens on this one!

## WALESBY

Walesby's name is said to suggest the presence of Welsh people in earlier settlements. As you walk towards the church, notice the lumpy ground in the fields; this was where the medieval Walesby stood. The village was also the site of a Roman villa, discovered in 1861. The famous All Saint's 'Rambler's church' on the hill overlooking the village makes a perfect resting place. Lying on the Viking Way, the thirteenth-century church has a colourful ramblers stained-glass window.

Also worthy of note are the Jacobean pulpit, box pews and an 'eccentric' 1930s rood screen. There are fine stone carvings on the pillar capitals, including some strange faces. The tower is buttressed at each corner as if against the winds, which can certainly blow here. The fourth-century font of an early Christian community was found in a nearby field in 1959 and the hilltop is thought to be the site of a Viking meeting place.

Thomas Malthus, the economist, whose theories regarding population were controversial, was once the rector. His book, *An Essay on the Principle of Population*, forewarned of the dangers of unrestricted population growth: 'The power of population is indefinitely greater than the power in the earth to produce subsistence for man.'

## TEALBY

Springs rising here feed the River Rase as it flows down from Bully Hill on its way towards Market Rasen. A village of chocolate box-cottages with roses around the door, it also has tea rooms and refreshments and is a good place to linger. The River Rase was important to Tealby, powering

# Kids' Stuff

**MAKE:**

**Your own motto.** Just like Caistor Grammar School has the motto, 'Always to Excel' and mine is 'It wasn't me', what will yours be?

**Cloud pictures.** Because we are on the highest ground in Lincolnshire and close to the sky, we should study it a little. Get everybody to lie on their backs and stare up at the clouds. Try to look for pictures in the clouds. To me they often look like seascapes with islands or faces. See what you can see!

**DESIGN:**
**An ungodly face!**

**FIND:**

**Some interesting rocks and fossils.** This is a good walk to start a collection of rocks and fossils. Just pick up small samples as you go and check them out at home to try to identify the type of rock, how old it is, how was it made and (if it's a fossil) what on earth is it and how old is it. Breaking open a piece of chalk and finding a fossil millions of years old that nobody else has ever seen or touched before is incomparable.

**LOOK UP:**
Buttress
Trig point
Pinnacle parapet
Bayons Manor. Check the Internet to find pictures of how this magnificent and strange stately home once looked.

its mills to grind the corn. It might seem quaint now but in its heyday in the 1850s it had up to six blacksmiths, and its own brickmaker. In the eighteenth century the mills also powered a papermaking industry.

All Saints church was built of local Tealby ironstone and 'disappointingly' restored in 1872. It has some fine stained glass. The tower has an embattled and pinnacled parapet and inside is a Norman font and many nineteenth-century memorials including one to George and Mary, Tennyson's grandparents. There are also some interesting eighteenth-century gravestones in the churchyard.

Following the Viking Way south out of Tealby, one crosses a ford which floods in heavy rain and further up the hill, behind the modern bungalow and band of trees to your left, were the romantic ruins of Bayons Manor. This was built by Charles Tennyson d'Eyncourt between 1836 and 1840. He was the MP for Lambeth and Tennyson's uncle, who discovered a loose and distant connection to the d'Eyncourt family and so added this to his name. Described by Thorold and Yates as an 'amazing building', old photographs reveal this to be an understatement. Part Regency, part Gothic, the sixty-room pile boasted a hall, library and tower and was surrounded by a large castellated wall, with 'formidable' gateways and numerous bastions, a moat and drawbridge.

Yates and Thorold tell us that to get to the front door you had to 'make a complete circuit of the defences'. Just to top it off they built a ruined keep behind it. After years of falling into disrepair, it was finally demolished with explosives in 1964 and the parkland ploughed up. What a loss to the county!

_____ *Further Reading*

Barley, M.W., *Lincolnshire and the Fens* (Batsford; London, 1952)

Carr, C., 'Portrait of a Village; Tealby' in *Lincolnshire Life* (c.1967)

Russell, R. and E. Holmes, *Two Hundred Years of Claxby Parish History* (Claxby Parish Council, 2002)

www.claxby.org.uk/history/history.pdf

www.caistor.net

Yates, J. and H. Thorold, *Lincolnshire: A Shell Guide* (Faber and Faber; London, 1965)

# A TRAMP ACROSS THE TOP OF THE WOLDS

From Horncastle to Louth

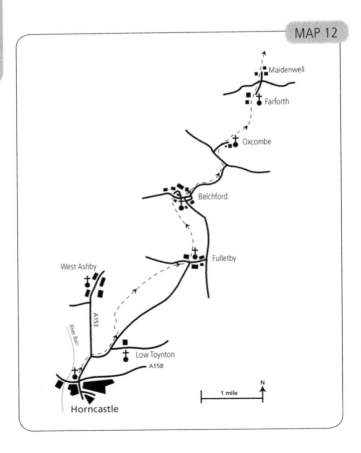

MAP 12

Maidenwell

Farforth

Oxcombe

Belchford

Fulletby

West Ashby

River Bain

A153

Low Toynton

A158

1 mile

N

Horncastle

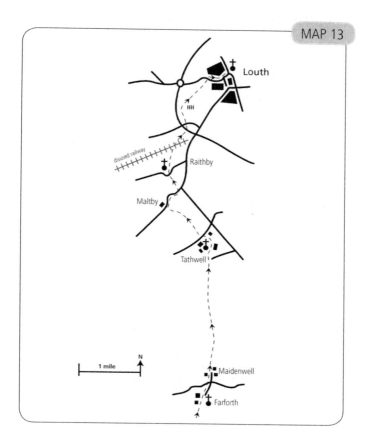

MAP 13

This is a classic 14-mile walk, linking the market town of Horncastle with the capital of the Wolds, Louth. Start at Louth, where there is plenty of parking, get an early bus to Horncastle and simply walk back. With good paths all the way, the route is varied and has much to offer in the way of history, wildlife, church architecture and stunning Wold views. The route links together sections of three other walks in this book to make up the town-to-town route. There is something satisfying, akin to a pilgrimage, in making such a journey, especially when you end up at the cathedral of the Wolds. The walk follows the Viking Way out of Horncastle to Belchford before heading towards Oxcombe, Farforth and Maidenwell, where it heads directly north to Tathwell and Raithby. It finally enters Louth through the beauty spot of Hubbards Hills. The details of most of the walk are given elsewhere, so here we just concentrate upon the thus far unexplored section between Maidenwell and Raithby. The whole walk rates a Grade 5 because of its length and after rain it can be hard going, especially if the fields have just been ploughed.

Maidenwell is said to be haunted by a coach and horses which appears as if out of a mist, driven by a coachman whose head lies on the seat next to him. You have been warned!

## MAIDENWELL

Maidenwell is basically a T-junction and a farm, which makes you wonder how it had a population of fifty-nine in 1870! It is reached after having walked through Oxcombe and Farforth in one of the nicest and least-known valleys in Lincolnshire. Folklore has it that Bonnie Prince Charlie stayed in Maidenwell in 1744 after landing at Saltfleet, en route to restore the Stuarts to the British throne. Apparently he stayed a couple of weeks and during that time attended a masked ball in Lincoln. However, the truth lies elsewhere, as his attempted 'invasion' in 1744 was scuppered by a storm in the Channel and he did not arrive in Britain until he landed on Eriskay in the Outer Hebrides in 1745.

From Maidenwell you pass a large grain store and drying barn out onto the Wolds, where there are panoramic views all around. The fields here are huge. You are walking parallel to the Greenwich Meridian, which is half a mile to the east and runs right through the centre of Louth.

## TATHWELL

This pretty village has a lake and springs which are the source of the River Lud and its name more or less means 'toad-spring'. The church, dedicated to St Vedast, is in a beautiful setting overlooking the lake. St Vedast was a French bishop who died in AD 540. He once stopped a wolf from stealing a goose, and so is often shown with these two animals. The oldest parts of the church, the base of the tower, date from the twelfth century, but the rest was rebuilt in brick in 1778. In the churchyard is a marble pillar to one Lord William Henry Cavendish Bentinck, who built and lived in Tathwell Lodge.

Be sure to notice the handmade bricks in the south-east corner and the heads by the church doorway (St Vedast is on the right).

Inside there is much of interest, such as a Victorian painting and a stained-glass window with a depiction of St Vedast with the goose and wolf. There is also an Anglo-Saxon grave slab but the church is largely noted for its numerous monuments to the local gentry, the Hambys and the Chaplins. One is a huge, four-storey alabaster creation from 1627, depicting the whole Hamby family in various poses. William (who instructed it to be

made) is at the top, beneath him are his brother Edward and his wife, and below these two are their seven daughters and six sons. All are kneeling on cushions and some are carrying skulls, one clearly a baby.

The Hambys had produced no male heir two generations later (not for want of trying!) and so the estate and lands passed to the Chaplin family, when granddaughter Elizabeth married a Francis Chaplin. On the opposite wall is a lovely marble panel, part of a monument to one Thomas Chaplin.

Another tablet tells us that Jane Chaplin lived to 102, which was pretty good going, especially in those days.

## MALTBY

Here notice the bumpy fields which indicate the site of the medieval village (which was wiped out by the plague in the fourteenth century). You can clearly see raised rectangles that show the outlines of the cottages.

# Kids' Stuff

**MAKE:**

**A trail stick.** A pilgrimage such as this demands a trail stick.

**A photo map.** This idea requires an eye for a good picture. You need to take a picture of the walk in front of you as far as you can see. Then, when you get to that point, you take another and so on. When you get the pictures printed, you make a long collage of them showing the journey.

**DRAW:**

**A walk badge.** Because it is a long way (over half a marathon) and something of a pilgrimage, the walk also deserves its own badge. So along the way gather ideas and as you stop to rest each time begin to draw your badge so that by the end of the walk you have the complete design. One idea is to make it shield shaped with quarters, with each having a different logo or design in.

**The Maidenwell ghost.** Don't forget the mist!

# THE ISLE OF AXHOLME

## A Strange Game and the Curious 'Tomb Preaching Incident'

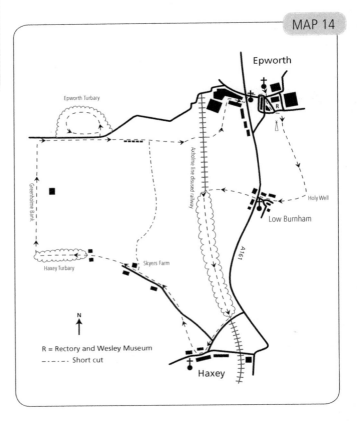

MAP 14

Epworth

Epworth Turbary

Axholme line disused railway

Greenholme Bank

Holy Well

Low Burnham

A161

Haxey Turbary

Skyers Farm

N

R = Rectory and Wesley Museum
— · — · — Short cut

Haxey

This 11-mile trail begins in the car park just below St Andrew's church in Epworth, the home of the preacher John Wesley, whose heritage is explored. The trail passes a holy well and Low Burnham before following a disused railway line nature reserve into Haxey, the home of the famous 'Hood' game! We then wander at sea level across the 'carrs', taking in two Turbury nature reserves, before returning to Epworth. A shortcut is indicated on the map and if you have small children with you it might be worth exploring Epworth, Haxey and their respective Turburys separately. The route, though flat and fairly easy, gets a Grade 4 for its length and, in parts, its bogginess.

## THE AXHOLME REVOLUTION

The Isle of Axholme is roughly 10 miles by 15 and was, until it was drained, an area of low lying, frequently flooded bog and marshland bounded by the rivers Trent, Idle and Don. It long preserved its independent identity. In the Civil War, for example, the folk of Axholme flooded the land to repel the king's army and also stubbornly refused Cromwell's attempts to reclaim the lands they had appropriated. Seems they hated interference in local affairs from any quarter.

Of Epworth, Shannon suggests that 'scarcely one acre of its black soil has had a peaceful history', alluding to the struggles against drainage and enclosure. When these spectres reared their heads and people lost their lands in the 1600s, there were violent protests. So much so that several of the leaders of the Levellers moved here to try and take over the leadership of what they saw, in Rogers' words, as a 'promising revolutionary movement'. Rivers were straightened and dykes cut to help the drainage, but the efforts of the dispossessed rioters undid most of this work. Eventually the land did get drained but one should pay due homage to this often overlooked bunch of revolting yellowbellies! To achieve this drainage, King Charles I engaged the Dutch engineer Cornelius Vermuyden in 1626 and up to 60,000 acres were subsequently drained with miles of ditches and the diversion of the rivers Don and Idle.

## EPWORTH AND WESLEY

Yates and Thorold tell us how one local squire described Epworth as the 'Lourdes of Methodism'. John Wesley, the non-conformist preacher, was born here in 1703 (one of nineteen offspring!) and his father held the parish for thirty-nine years. In the town square you can see the remains of the market cross from which he used to preach, and next to which

many have posed for Wesley-type portraits. The church of St Andrew is Early English, with a perpendicular tower and is set on a small hill. Inside it has a twelfth-century font used to baptise Wesley and there are some fine stained-glass windows by W.H. Constable, a relative of the artist John Constable. The main pillars in the nave are leaning alarmingly outwards and just to the left of the porch outside are parts of a medieval tombstone which could have belonged to a crusader. Also outside is the 'Table Tomb' of his father Samuel Wesley, upon which John is said to have stood to preach after being refused permission to preach inside.

This area of Lincolnshire had a long tradition of independent religious thought and this must have been a strong influence upon Wesley Junior. Wesley saw the path to salvation as being primarily through discipline, and he devoted his life to preaching the word all over the land. He commonly used to preach at the market cross in Epworth and, as well as North Lincolnshire and the Wolds, he targeted large towns due to their high levels of poverty and crime. His preaching was passionate and Barley quotes Horace Walpole describing his style as having a 'very ugly enthusiasm'.

You can imagine the effect of this 'ugliness' in a small Wolds town, where the congregation numbered a few dozen farm labourers, the local gentry and the lord of the manor and his kin. Wesley's father was relatively poor and whilst at Oxford University Wesley once walked all the way home, obviously an early disciple of the Long Distance Walkers Association! He is remembered today the world over as the founder of the Methodist Church. The Old Rectory, a Queen Anne building, is open to visitors in season (closed Sundays) and contains much memorabilia and insights into Wesley and should not be bypassed.

In 1716, banging on the front door and other strange unexplained phenomena occurred at the Old Rectory, occupied by the Wesley family. They became so regular that one set of footsteps was named 'Old Jeffrey'. One other poltergeist which had set up residence appeared as an old man in a white gown running up and down the stairs and levitating beds. This was no shy ghost.

The 1889 Wesley Memorial Methodist church is also worth a visit when you come back into Epworth, if only to see the fine stained-glass portrait of John and Charles Wesley.

## LOW BURNHAM

Leaving Epworth via the track almost opposite the rectory, you head for Low Burnham and just before getting there come upon the 'Holy Well', an area of boggy ground and the site of a spring said to possess the power of healing, provided you were dipped in the waters before noon! Crossing the A161 you take the lane opposite Low Burnham Methodist Chapel to connect with the Axholme line disused railway.

## AXHOLME LINE

About 1½ miles of the disused Axholme light railway is a nature reserve which takes us into Haxey. Cutting through alkaline mudstone, there is a good range of plant species including orchids, and in season this is a wonderful place for seeing a large number of butterfly species.

## HAXEY

A Bronze Age gold torc (neck ring) dating back about 3,000 years was found near Haxey and now resides in the British Museum, but our friends Yates and Thorold are less enamoured with the place, calling it 'a decayed little town of red houses'. This is a bit harsh as it does have some charm. They do concede that St Nicholas' church is 'dignified' and is referred to as 'the cathedral of the Isle'. It has an eight-pinnacle tower and a large and airy Norman nave, a fine chancel and some impressive stained glass, particularly the Faith, Hope and Charity window in the south aisle. The church itself is perched on a small isle slightly raised above the surrounding flood plain. Outside is the Mowbray stone, from whence the annual battle known as the Haxey Hood commences.

## THE HAXEY HOOD

'Hoose agen hoose, toon agen toon, if tha meets a man nok im doon, but doant 'ot im'.

There you have it, the rules! This is a serious affair and is presided over by a fool and twelve referees or 'Boggans' (ploughboys of old). This 700-year-old tradition is played on the Twelfth Day of Christmas (i.e. 6th January unless this is a Sunday, when it is played on the 5th). Legend has it that

a lady lost her scarf or hood in the wind and thirteen labourers chased after it in the hope of retrieving it. Today the hood is fought over by locals, trying to get it back to a local pub in either Haxey or the neighbouring village of Westwoodside. So it is a beautiful game unsullied by rules other than the words above, which are uttered by the fool from the Mowbray stone whilst being smoked like a kipper ... well why not? The hood is cast into the air and it is every man for himself as the 'sway' slowly makes progress over muddy ground. Think of a slow, muddy, huge rugby scrum probably lasting all day and you have a fairly accurate picture. At the end, somewhere in the area a pub has the hood; what an excuse for a drink – 'I'm just going to look for the hood'.

Life on the land 700 years ago was hard in this area, with many livelihoods threatened by drainage or enclosure, so such traditions provided a much-needed diversion. The hood today is a tight roll of cloth and 'kick off' is usually at 2 p.m. (after a few stiffening drinks), but don't worry about being late as it often goes on well into the evening.

# Kids' Stuff

## WATCH:

**Butterflies and dragonflies.** This is a good walk to concentrate on both butterflies and dragonflies. The dry disused railway cuttings will let you get close to butterflies and the Turburys will let you get nearly as close to dragonflies. Try using a good camera with a zoom lens to get pictures and try your fieldcraft techniques, creeping up slowly and quietly. Lookout for other stuff too, as on the last walk I did here I saw a polecat/ferret and a grass snake!

## MAKE:

**Some bark rubbings.** You just need a sheet of paper and wax crayons. Rub the bark and try and get a leaf too. Then when back at home identify the tree and make your tree bark identity guide.

**A dream catcher or wind chime.** Just collect various objects during the walk and string them together when you get home.

## DESIGN:

**A village game.** The Haxey Hood is a great competition to have in the village. Think about where you live and come up with your own weird game. Keep the rules to a minimum – the less sense it makes and dirtier it is the better.

## HAXEY AND EPWORTH TURBURYS

These are rare relicts of raised bog in an area which has been extensively cut for peat. As such they hold fine examples of key species, such as sphagnum moss, cotton grass, purple loose-strife and cross-leaved heath. Specialist species include fen sedge and royal fern. Birch scrub is encroaching on the wet heath and bog and this attracts breeding birds such as tree pipits and warblers. The reserves are particularly good for dragonflies. On summer afternoons, at Epworth in particular, look out for hobbies chasing dragonflies, catching them with their feet and then eating them on the wing. An early morning or late evening visit may well repay you with a sighting of woodcock 'roding' and this is a beautiful time to visit this site. Because all around the land is being drained with a vengeance, the reserve management plan concentrates on keeping the water levels high and holding back the invasive birch. When visiting in winter or after heavy rain, wellingtons will be a good idea!

*Further Reading*

Codd, S., *Haunted Lincolnshire* (Tempus; Stroud, 2006)

Rogers, A., *A History of Lincolnshire* (Phillmore; Chichester, 1985)

Shannon, I., 'The Isle of Axholme' in *Lincolnshire Life* (Vol. 5, No. 4, August/September 1965)

www.epwortholdrectory.org.uk

# THE ALKBOROUGH CIRCUIT

## An 'Amazing' Walk by Trent and Humber

This 9-mile walk centres on the village of Alkborough, overlooking the point at which the rivers Ouse, Trent and Humber meet. A turf maze called Julian's Bower is explored before walking along the sea wall to the Trent outfall and through Alkborough Flats bird reserve on the way to Whitton, where we rest at the Norman church. The circuit heads back in along the 'cliff'(!) to Alkborough church. The route starts at Julian's Bower, where you can park on the road. The walk is a Grade 2 with easy going and route finding.

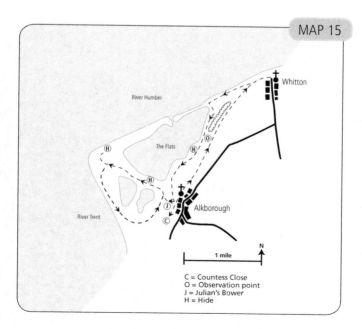

MAP 15

Whitton

River Humber

The Flats

Alkborough

River Trent

N

1 mile

C = Countess Close
O = Observation point
J = Julian's Bower
H = Hide

## ALKBOROUGH

There are superb views from Julian's Bower across Alkborough Flats to the Trent Falls, so called because you are looking at the spot where the Trent falls into the Humber along with the Ouse: a meeting of three rivers. Alkborough was called 'Alchebarge' in Domesday Book and in medieval times there was a port of sorts at the point where our walk meets the Trent bank. Yates and Thorold, in their usual dry style, claimed the village had a 'Yorkshire bleakness', but you may think otherwise.

## JULIAN'S BOWER

This is a rare turf maze dating back to we know not when, but it is first recorded in the late seventeenth century. It is circular and consists of a raised turf path cut into the cliff. Such mazes are often called Julian's Bower and are said to be named after Julius, the son of Aeneas, the founder of Rome, who apparently brought the tradition back from Troy.

In the twelfth century there was a Benedictine farmstead here and some believe that the church adapted the maze to serve as a 'trail of penance' along the 'path to salvation' whereby you had to walk the lengthy path to the central cross with stones in your shoes!

## PLOUGH JAG PLAY

Barley suggests that the maze might also have become a site for traditional games, such as the Plough Jag Play, which he claims was a strong tradition in Alkborough. Plough Jags are ploughboys and the play was performed on Plough Monday, the first Monday after Twelfth Night. In the late nineteenth century the play was mixed with folk songs, decorated top hats, a Hobby Horse and morris dancing, and toured around the village.

Walk 200 metres south of the maze towards Burton Stather and you will find Countess Close or the Aquis of Ravenas, the site of a Roman castle or 'castrum'. It is 300 square feet and overlooks the Trent, a superb defensive and lookout position, with the movements of those across the water being easily monitored. You can see the remains of the vallum (ramparts) and ditch. Later archaeological opinion suggests that it is in fact the remains of a medieval manor house.

Our route heads down to the Flats from the Bower.

## ALKBOROUGH FLATS

In Autumn 2006 the flood bank of the Humber estuary was intentionally breached, flooding acres of farmland and restoring some of the Humber's natural flood control plains. However, part of the plan was also the creation of a superb nature reserve that has already become a haven for wildlife. The Flats are particularly good for wading birds and wildfowl, with an already impressive list of rarities to its name. The Humber is one of Europe's top destinations for migratory wildfowl, which flock here to fuel up on the vast intertidal mud flats, and there are several bird hides en route.

The Flats have Civil War connections, as in the mid-seventeenth century a small fort and gun battery were set up near the hide on the sea wall. Cromwell's troops ousted the Royalists stationed here. The path returns through the Flats and along their landward edge, eventually rejoining the sea wall before entering Whitton.

# WHITTON

This place has a remarkable sense of isolation, yet at one time it was served by the North Lindsey Light Railway and a glance at the map will show you the disused railway route. The railway came to Whitton in 1910 and was built to serve the iron ore industry at Scunthorpe, the ore being transferred to a cargo ferry to Hull.

In AD 71 the Romans forded the Humber just a couple of miles downriver from here at Winteringham, which was at the north end of the great Roman road Ermine Street, coming up from London through Lincoln on its way to York. After AD 400, the Vikings invaded these parts and one can conjure up images of fleets of longboats coming down the Humber and Trent, with the locals watching in trepidation. Later on, after William the Conqueror successfully invaded, Domesday Book valued Whitton and its lands at a mere £7!

The church of St John the Baptist originated as Norman and has a Norman font with lovely typical rounded Norman arches. There are large Roman stone blocks incorporated into the tower and Yates and Thorold commented that this Norman tower gives a 'sense of stubborn resistance to invaders'.

Leaving Whitton, the path takes the cliff top route back to Alkborough. Take a good look in the fields by the path and you will find literally hundreds of 'Devil's toenails'.

In more recent times, the Flats which spread out below us now were used as a bombing range in the Second World War. An observation post is all that remains now, which makes a good spot for a breather.

# ALKBOROUGH

Back in Alkborough, the church of St John the Baptist has the remains of an ancient cross which is partially worn away by sword and scythe sharpening in medieval times.

The Saxon tower dates from before the Norman conquests. It is alleged that three of the knights who murdered Thomas Beckett in Canterbury Cathedral (Hugo Morville, William Tracy and Reginald Fitzurse) rebuilt the church as an act of contrition. However, the inscribed stone bearing testimony to this, reported in 1697, is lost in time! The oak reredos behind the altar was handmade by the famous Robert (Mouseman)

# Kids' Stuff

**DESIGN:**
**A maze.** Draw it on paper and be sure to put in lots of dead endings.

**PLAY:**
**Bird racing.** From the beginning of the walk you shout out (quietly) the name of the bird you spot. This gives you the point and no one else can get a point from that species. The next person to see a different species first gets the next point and so on. The first person to 10 wins.

**Egg carton mysteries!** Each person carries an egg carton with them and during the walk they have to put something in all six egg spaces. It has to be something that you are not sure what it is. When you get home you get on with the serious business of identifying your hoard.

**Photo Bamboozling.** Take a camera out with you and take pictures of unusual objects or strange views and extreme close ups of common objects. Then when you get home download them onto your computer and hold a guess what it is quiz. This is a great way to relive the walk again when you get home.

**FIND:**
**The Mouseman's mouse.** Somewhere on the reredos of Alkborough church hides Thompson's mouse signature.

**The biggest Devil's toenail.**

Thompson of Kilburn. See if you can find his signature mouse. There is also a copy of the bower maze cut into the church porch floor and another in one of the stained-glass windows. It is also on the gravestone of James Constable in the churchyard.

*Further Reading*

Barley, M.W., *Lincolnshire and the Fens* (Batsford; London, 1952)
Allen, Thomas, Assisted by several gentlemen residing in the county eminent either for their Literary abilities or their extensive local knowledge, *The History of the County of Lincoln* (John Saunders Junior; London and Lincoln, 1834)
Yates, J. and H. Thorold, *Lincolnshire; A Shell Guide* (Faber and Faber; London, 1965)
www.south-humber-collection.org
www.diplomate.freeserve.co.uk/whitton.htm – This site gives a good history of Whitton

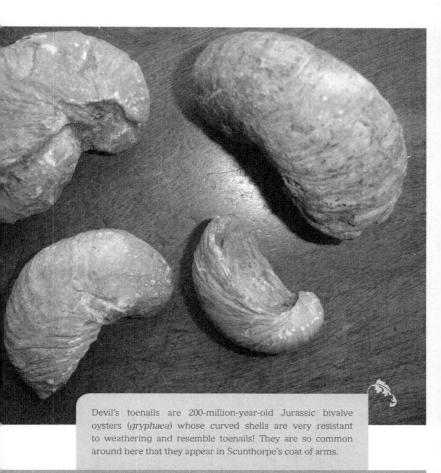

Devil's toenails are 200-million-year-old Jurassic bivalve oysters (*gryphaea*) whose curved shells are very resistant to weathering and resemble toenails! They are so common around here that they appear in Scunthorpe's coat of arms.

# THE HUMBER BRIDGE, BRICKS, BARTON AND BIRDS

This walk is one that embraces modern heritage in a quite spectacular way. The Humber Bridge is an iconic monument to modern engineering and an extremely different walking experience, needing a good head for heights! The Humber estuary is also an important and impressive natural feature, so

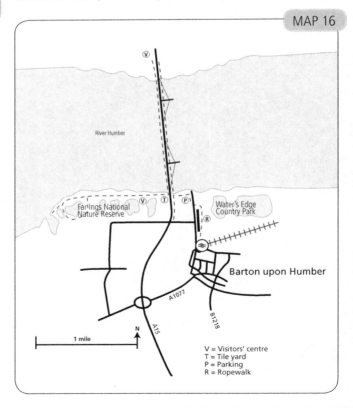

MAP 16

River Humber

Far Ings National Nature Reserve

Water's Edge Country Park

Barton upon Humber

A1077

A15

B1218

1 mile

N

V = Visitors' centre
T = Tile yard
P = Parking
R = Ropewalk

we combine the bridge with a circuit of Far Ings National Nature Reserve. The walk also connects with the ancient art of brickmaking and tours Barton upon Humber, a fine town steeped in history wherever you look and boasting Lincolnshire's finest Saxon church.

The walk can be undertaken in one 10-mile jaunt, but I'd suggest breaking it down. There are three loops from the car park at Barton Waterside (Far Ings 3 miles, bridge and Barton 4 miles each) and it is worth taking your time to explore Barton on its own in a day. The bridge and Far Ings can be combined into a 6-mile walk. The going is easy unless a gale is blowing across the bridge and you are not good with heights, but otherwise this walk rates a Grade 2.

## BOUNDARIES

It was very nearly impossible to include this walk, due to an anomaly in our political heritage. In 1974, local government reorganisation created the county of Humberside, slicing off the top of Lincolnshire; 300,000 yellowbellies came perilously close to becoming quasi Yorkshiremen! This reorganisation took out Grimsby, Scunthorpe, Immingham, Brigg and Epworth, the birthplace of Wesley. Despite much local opposition, the politicians had their day and seemed to think that the opposite banks of the Humber had some sort of natural affinity. For many, this was somewhat akin to suggesting that Liverpool and Everton should merge. Common sense eventually prevailed and on 1 April 1996, Humberside was abolished and Lincolnshire reunited.

## HUMBER BRIDGE

Eight years in the making, the first traffic crossed the bridge on 24 June 1981, Queen Elizabeth II having performed the opening ceremony on 17 June.

The statistics are mind-boggling. When it was built, the bridge was the longest single-span suspension bridge in the world at 4,626 feet (1,410 metres). The total length between the anchorage points is 7,284 feet (2,220 metres) or 1.38 miles. The main cables are 2 feet 3 inches (0.68 metres) thick and in total there is 71,000 kilometres of cable (44,117 miles). The towers are 510 feet (155.5 metres) high and the bridge is basically 27,500 tonnes of steel and 480,000 tonnes of concrete, with the water being 98 feet (30 metres) below you as you cross. By the end of 2011 it had carried 158,777,658 vehicles! Make sure you visit the information centre at the north end of the bridge and pick up the leaflets outlining even more staggering statistics.

On the way across, take time to ponder the engineering brilliance of this monument and look down at the Humber in full flow. Looking at the bridge from the car park, I'd suggest walking out along the right-hand side and back along the left.

## BRICK WORKS AND TILERIES

The Humber is one of Britain's largest estuaries and an internationally important area for birdlife; its vast areas of mud exposed at low tide provide vital feeding grounds for thousands of waders in winter, and in migration periods it attracts many rarer species. As you walk back across the bridge towards the south shore, note the tileries below you. Blyth's tile yard, whose square chimney you can see, was one of fifteen back in 1900. It is set to become a tile heritage and craft centre. Clay underlies the local area and since Roman times this has been put to good use in making bricks and tiles. Into the nineteenth century there were still many brick and tile yards here. In this area you have both the raw material and a ready means of transport, and the clay here was of high enough quality to make tiles and chimney pots as well as bricks.

## FAR INGS

The word 'Ings' means wet grassland and is typically applied to land which becomes waterlogged in winter, which often happened before banks were constructed along the Humber. As we have seen, the underlying clay was exploited and as the clay pits were exhausted and abandoned, they quickly filled with water and became colonised with water-loving plants such as reed and willow. Luckily, the wildlife value of these pits was recognised and the Lincolnshire Wildlife Trust got hold of them. This is why membership of such groups is so important in preserving our wildlife heritage; without habitat there is no wildlife.

One of the highlights of the Ings is its contribution to the welcome return from the brink of extinction of one of Britain's rarest birds, the bittern. Without the Ings there would be no reeds and without the reeds there would be no bitterns. This is a fascinating bird, superbly camouflaged in the reeds and with a remarkable 'booming' call that can carry for miles, eerie on a foggy day and sounding much like a foghorn. The Ings is a great place for birdwatching all year round, with an abundance of wildfowl to be seen, and the visitor centre has interpretive displays so you can check out those you are not sure of.

## BARTON UPON HUMBER

The word Barton derives from 'Beretun' meaning 'Barley Farm', so it has been a farming community for a very long time. The Romans commanded a 'ford' just west of Barton, where it was possible to walk across the Humber at low tide. Later in medieval times, Barton was the most important port on the Humber, but it was eventually usurped by Hull.

Daniel Defoe, travelling in the late seventeenth century, described Barton as a town 'noted for nothing that I know of, but an ill favoured dangerous passage, or ferry, over the Humber to Hull'. His passage was in an open boat shared with horses and cows and they were 'four hours tossed about' until they could get into the harbour at Hull. What a difference a bridge makes! The last ferry from Barton to Hull left in 1851, usurped by a ferry from New Holland which itself went to the wall in 1981 when the bridge opened.

From the bridge car park we cross the Haven Bridge and walk on into Barton to explore its heritage. The old coastguard station by the car park also marks the start of the long distance footpath the Viking Way, which wanders across Lincolnshire and ends up at Oakham in Rutland some 140 miles away.

As you walk around the town you will notice a plethora of superb Georgian and Victorian buildings, each with its own story to tell. I can only touch upon some of them here.

## ROPEWALK

Barton also used to be a centre for ropemaking and the quarter-mile-long 'Ropewalk' building (established 1767) was the heart of this. It was particularly busy during the two world wars. The factory closed in 1989 and today it is an arts and crafts venue, coffee shop and concert hall. Inside is a fine exhibition relating to its rope-making past.

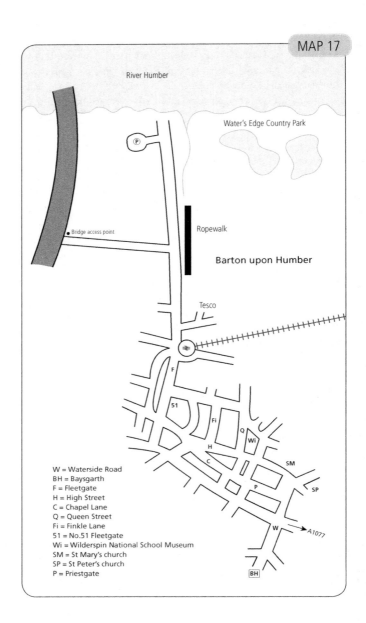

MAP 17

River Humber

Water's Edge Country Park

P

Ropewalk

Bridge access point

Barton upon Humber

Tesco

F

51

Fi

Q

Wi

H

C

SM

P

SP

W = Waterside Road
BH = Baysgarth
F = Fleetgate
H = High Street
C = Chapel Lane
Q = Queen Street
Fi = Finkle Lane
51 = No.51 Fleetgate
Wi = Wilderspin National School Museum
SM = St Mary's church
SP = St Peter's church
P = Priestgate

W

A1077

BH

## NO. 51 FLEETGATE

Barton Civic Society looks after this building that dates back to 1325, reputed to be the oldest residential house in North Lincolnshire. The Clipson family bought it in 1908 and turned it into a barbers and tobacconists and it has remained relatively unchanged ever since. You will need to check online for its open days.

## WILDERSPIN NATIONAL SCHOOL MUSEUM

These preserved Victorian schoolrooms were the work of educational pioneer Samuel Wilderspin in 1844. Wilderspin changed the face of primary schools and this one was designed for the use of infants from the age of 2 to 6. As well as the schoolroom and playground, you can wonder at the ten 'headed' shared toilet! Wilderspin's biggest contribution was in recognising the importance of play and instigating the 'playground' concept.

Just over the road is a charity school built in 1831, whose first master was non other than Isaac Pitman, the inventor of shorthand. This sober street also houses a temperance hall and the Salvation Army, and just around the corner in the High Street is the old police station.

## ST MARY'S CHURCH

Dating back to the twelfth century, this church once came under the jurisdiction of St Peter's, but it remains unclear as to why there should be two churches in such close proximity. It has both a Romanesque aisle and a Gothic aisle. The tower was added in the thirteenth century and the clerestory in the fifteenth. There are several small chapels in the church with much to look for, but notice in particular the carved faces between the arches. One of these is reminiscent of the Lincoln Imp, with a devil's face and long cow-like ears. Also look out for the foliage on the wooden screens and the Green Man carved into the stone pillars. By the altar, look at the brass on the floor of Simon Seman, a local man who became a vintner in London. His feet rest on two wine barrels and at the corners are the symbols of Matthew (angel), Mark (lion), Luke (ox) and John (eagle). Outside notice the bizarre church sign, somewhat reminiscent of Munch's *The Scream*.

Just a stone's throw from St Mary's, this church has a complete Anglo-Saxon tower and baptistery dating from around 970. Its nave and chancel are medieval. Excavations here uncovered 2,800 burials from Anglo-Saxon to Victorian times, giving us a remarkable insight into the

# Kids' Stuff

**PLAY:**

**I spy cars.** List as many different types of car as you can whilst crossing the bridge.

**A weirdest bridge photo competition.** Take the cameras and try and get some unusual angle shots of the bridge, such as looking along a cable, or up a pillar or down to the water on top of a passing boat. Be careful not to drop the camera over the side!

**MAKE:**

**Your own impressive statistic.** Count how many steps it takes you to get from one side of the bridge to the other.

**WATCH:**

**For birds.** This is a good place to see some of our more elusive birds, such as bittern and water rail. A summer list of twenty to tick off is: Great crested grebe, bittern, water rail, pochard, tufted duck, shoveler, heron, snipe, common tern, avocet, redshank, kingfisher, marsh harrier, sedge warbler, reed warbler, chiffchaff, swallow, sand martin, tree sparrow, reed bunting.

**LOOK UP:**

**Just exactly how was the bridge built?** Check out www.humberbridge. co.uk/media/Engineering_The_Humber_Bridge_e-book.pdf

lives of those who lived here, including such aspects as diet and medical practices.

There is an exhibition in the church which is in the care of English Heritage. Just inside the tower, above the arch, notice the tenth-century carved face of Christ; it is not often you get to see such a rare work. There are also some superbly carved fourteenth-century Green Men with foliage sprouting from their mouths at the top of the pillars.

Notice, too, the wall monument to Sir John Nelthorpe of Baysgarth House. The son of one of St Peter's vicars was Chad Varah, who was the founder of the Samaritans. Outside look for the grave of 'Christmas Johnson' and six children who died in infancy but remain nameless.

## BAYSGARTH HOUSE MUSEUM

This is the ancestral home of the Nelthorpe family and is a superb example of Georgian architecture. Sir John Nelthorpe was painted by Stubbs with Barton in the background and it now houses a museum relating to many things Barton-esque. There is also an industrial museum in the old stable block that examines the local crafts and industry of Barton area.

--------------------------------- *Further Reading*

Defoe, D., *A Tour Thro' the Whole Island of Great Britain* (Penguin; Harmondsworth, 1724)
www.english-heritage.org.uk
www.lincstrust.org.uk

# LINCOLN

A Stroll Around the Past and
a Jaw-Dropping Tribute
to Craftsmen of Old

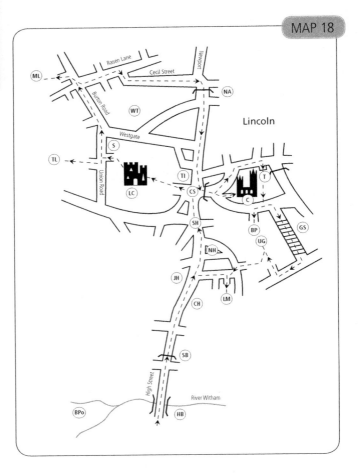

MAP 18

Rasen Lane

Cecil Street

Newport

ML

NA

Lincoln

WT

Burton Road

Westgate

S

TL

Union Road

TI

LC

CS

T

C

SH

BP

GS

UG

NH

JH

LM

CH

SB

High Street

River Witham

BPo

HB

This is the shortest walk in the book at 3 miles, but it will likely take you the longest time to complete because it covers a lot of heritage in a small area. It is better to do it over two days and take your time to enjoy it rather than rush. I have chosen 'uphill' Lincoln's best bits and give you a suggested route covering all twenty features mentioned, but as you wander around you will come across many more aspects and features well worthy of exploration and admiration. There is not space to discuss all the features of the places on the route – that would take a book of its own – so just use this as a rough guide with 'don't miss' suggestions, and the castle, Bishop's Palace and cathedral have their own very comprehensive guidebooks should you want to read more.

The letters in brackets below denote the features location on the map. There is plenty of parking in the town centre and the walk is a mere Grade 1 (if you ignore the fact that it climbs a Grade 5 hill, which catches the tourists unawares, thinking as they do, that Lincolnshire is flat!).

## HIGH BRIDGE (HB)

The High Bridge is a twelfth-century structure and the oldest bridge in Britain to still carry buildings. The three-storey timber-framed buildings straddle the River Witham as it leaves Brayford Pool (BPo), on its way to the Wash at Boston. The High Street follows the line of the Roman Ermine Street, now several feet below. Sneak down the steps by the side of the building and take a quick look at the Brayford. Natural pools were dug out by the Romans to create an inland port, albeit 40 miles from the sea. They then dug the Fosse Dyke linking the Witham to the Trent so you could sail from the Wash, up the Witham to the Brayford, out along the Fosse to the Trent and from here on up to York. Or down the Humber and back down to the Wash and round again. Coming back, the view of the rear and underneath the bridge is a fine sight when filled with the town's many mute swans that once supplied the courts of Henry III. This is known as the 'Glory Hole'. Opposite on the other side of the bridge there used to be a small chapel of St Thomas, sadly no longer in existence.

## THE STONEBOW (SB)

This archway was built on the site of a Roman gateway and then rebuilt as the southern gate of the medieval city, completed in 1520, which subsequently had the Lincoln Guildhall built over it. Lincoln's council meet here and it houses the city regalia, such as the mayor's ring, chain

A favourite trick of Lincoln dwellers is to inform their non-local friends that they would meet them on the clock side of the Stonebow, which of course has a clock on both sides.

of office and his maces. Traffic flowed through it and down the High Street until 1973.

## THE CARDINAL'S HAT (CH)

With Dernstall House next door, these are fine examples of Tudor half-timbered houses, leaning out over the street. Cardinal Wolsey was Bishop of Lincoln in 1514.

## JEWS HOUSE (JH)

Said by some to be the oldest occupied house in England, it was built around 1160 at a time when few houses were built of stone. Its name derives from the fact that, at one time, it was owned by a Jewish woman who was executed for allegedly 'clipping' coins, but more likely linked to the general expulsion of the Jews from England in the late thirteenth century. Today it houses the Society for Lincolnshire History and Archaeology and its bookshop. Note the arches of the door and upper windows.

## NORMAN HOUSE (NH)

Dating from around 1170, it was thought to have once been the home of one Aaron, a wealthy Jewish moneylender whose money helped finance the building of several cathedrals, including Lincoln's. This is now disputed but it remains a fine example of a medieval house. The restored 1878 double window is worthy of note, as this is how such Norman windows would have looked. We now climb up Steep Hill (SH) into Castle Square (CS).

## TOURIST INFORMATION OFFICE (TI)

Built around 1543, Leigh-Pemberton House (to give it its full title) looks the classic Tudor timber-framed building. It has been a merchant's house, inn and, up until 1979, a bank, but now serves appropriately as a Tourist Information Centre. Robert Leigh-Pemberton was the Governor of the Bank of England, who gave the property to the city.

## LINCOLN CASTLE (LC)

The building of the castle was ordered by William the Conqueror in 1068 and it was built in a truly commanding position, overlooking the Witham and Trent basin. A castle needs towers and turrets and Lincoln has several. The Observatory Tower is crowned with a circular turret and gives great views over the town and the cathedral. The Lucy Tower is the keep, and is unusually built upon a second mound. It would have had lean-to buildings around the inner walls.

In the nineteenth century it was used as a burial ground for criminals and you will notice two rows of prisoners' graves, including two small graves of children who were born and died in the prison. A third tower, Cobb Hall, contains the dungeons, still with the iron rings to which prisoners were chained. Preserved on the walls are graffiti scratched in by those who were held here. Lincoln Crown Court is still situated and operates within the castle and the old Victorian gaol house (1787) is also on view. There is an intriguing chapel with individual interlocking cubicles, designed so that the prisoners can't see each other and are forced to look upon the preacher. The seats also slope down, so that you could not sit comfortably and had to half stand. Other things to look out for are the 'herring bone' stonework in the walls and just inside the east gateway is a beautiful Oriel window, moved here in 1849 from elsewhere in the city. One should also visit the original copy of Magna Carta, signed by King John in 1215.

## THE LAWNS (TL)

This was originally known as the Lincoln Asylum and opened in 1820 as the county's first psychiatric hospital. One of the asylum's major instigators was Dr Francis Willis, who attended King George III and was the subject of the film *The Madness of King George*. The hospital was first supervised by Dr E.P. Charlesworth, who pioneered 'restraint free' treatment, preferring 'attention', 'useful occupation' and 'entertainment'. Clients were put to such tasks as bookkeeping, laundry work, gardening, kitchen duties and encouraged to knit and make artificial flowers. There was also a monthly ball and visits to church, the castle and cathedral, fairs, concerts and the races.

Lying in the Lawns' grounds is the Joseph Banks Conservatory. This peaceful tropical glasshouse contains some of the plants discovered by Banks when he sailed with Captain Cook in the *Endeavour* on his voyage to discover Australia. The botanist was the son of a Lincolnshire landowner.

## THE STRUGGLERS (S)

This is real ale at its best in a thriving, award-winning local. The county gallows used to stand on this corner and the pub name refers to the reluctance of the condemned as they were dragged towards the scaffold.

## MUSEUM OF LINCOLNSHIRE LIFE (ML)

This 'cornucopia of yesteryear' is housed in an old army barracks, built in 1857 for the Royal North Lincoln Militia. They were part-time volunteers whose main role was home defence. The museum has a fascinating collection of items relating to social history, with many mocked-up rooms and shops from the past. There is also a focus on the history of the tank, which was developed by Fosters of Lincoln whose managing director, Sir William Tritton, was credited with its invention. It became an essential piece of military equipment for crossing the trenches in the First World War.

## WATER TOWER (WT)

Note the large square water tower in Westgate, built in 1911 after a tragic outbreak of typhoid in 1904–5 when 131 people died. It reputedly holds 300,000 gallons, enough to supply uphill Lincoln for a day!

## NEWPORT ARCH (NA)

The north gate of the Roman town, this is the best-preserved Roman gateway in Britain. Originally it would have been a small tunnel with a smaller arch on both sides, and outside these two defensive towers. Street levels have risen about 8 feet since Roman times, so it would have appeared much higher. It is still open to traffic and over the years has fallen victim to high vehicles, nearly being destroyed by a lorry in 1964.

## LINCOLN CATHEDRAL (C)

From a distance, standing proud 200 feet up on the limestone edge as you approach Lincoln, the cathedral looks hugely impressive. This feeling grows the nearer you get until, close up and hands on, one cannot fail to be moved and impressed by its sheer magnificence and the blood, sweat, tears and skill that went into building it. Yates and Thorold called the view of the cathedral from downhill, 'one of the great sights of Europe'. It has its major tourist features, as any cathedral does, but draw back from the crowd, find a quiet corner and just examine a piece of carved stone or wood. There are literally thousands of works of art here. Think pre-electric tools, pre-metal scaffolding, pre-JCB; think ropes and pulleys and flimsy wooden walkways high up and the building process itself become an art work of jaw-dropping wonder. Make sure that you climb the tower to take in the stunning views of the city and surrounding countryside. The tower was completed in 1131 and is 271 feet high. All three towers originally had spires and the central tower was once the tallest structure in Europe.

Outside, the west front takes some beating, especially the twelfth-century friezes depicting the tortures of Hell, Noah's ark and Daniel in the lion's den.

The Normans began building the cathedral in 1072 but it suffered a fire in 1141, and an earthquake in 1185 destroyed most of the Norman church. The remains of this early Norman church can still be seen in the arched doorways of the west front, and St Hugh began the rebuilding from 1192. The vast nave with its ribbed vaulting is supported by huge limestone and Purbeck marble pillars and it is dizzying to look up to the ceiling under the central tower and see how high above you it is.

Now look from left to right and you will see two round windows: the 'Bishop's Eye' and the 'Dean's Eye'. The leaf-shaped stone tracery of the Bishop's Eye window can be found nowhere else in the world. Built in the shape of a cross, the cathedral became slightly out of kilter when being rebuilt. Look back up the nave from the choir screen and see if you can tell. Arguably the finest features of the cathedral are the stalls of the choir.

# Kids' Stuff

**DESIGN:**

**Your own imp.**

**Your own castle, and then build it.** Draw a basic design and build a model of it out of thick cardboard then cover it with paper mache. Then paint it. Don't forget the drawbridge and moat!

**PLAY:**
**Hold an archery contest.** This of course must be held within the castle grounds.

**WATCH:**
*The Madness of King George.*

**MAKE:**
**Lincoln tarts.** These are easy to make:
Just mix 175g of flour with 2 tablespoons of sugar and a pinch of salt. Then chop up 75g of butter and rub it into the flour until it looks like breadcrumbs. Then add water and knead it until you have a bread-like consistency. Cut

out your pastry circles and put some red jam into them. Use more dough to make into imp shapes and place these in the centre of the tarts. Bake for 18 minutes at 200°C and allow to cool.

**A tank.** Use two matchsticks, a cotton reel and an elastic band. I am not going to tell you how; you will have to invent it yourself or ask someone pretty old!

**LISTEN:**
**To William Byrd.** He was the organist at Lincoln Cathedral in 1563.

They are superbly carved with symbols and figures of contemporary relevance. Whilst here, remember to lift a few seats up and examine the misericords and look up at the ceiling in St Hugh's choir to see the strange vaulting! Check out also two small owls looking from a capital of the doorway, just right of the choir screen, and see if you can spot the tiny owl on a capital of the choir screen itself. The quality of the carving on this stone screen is superb.

The south porch on the outside has some superb carving and the door depicts the Day of Judgement, with a central Christ surrounded by angels and souls, either being dragged down in to Hell by demons or saved. By the porch is a marvellous statue of Edward I and his wife Eleanor, whilst nearby is one of his second wife Marguerite de Valois. The cathedral also houses several tombs of note. Apart from the shrine to St Hugh, there is a Victorian tomb where Eleanor of Castile's entrails are buried and the tomb of Catherine Swynford, third wife of John of Gaunt. The chapter house supported by its central pillar is magnificent in its own right. Look at the stained-glass windows and see if you can spot the panel depicting the earthquake and fire that destroyed the early cathedral. Outside you will see the splendid flying buttresses propping it up.

Perhaps the cathedral's most famous feature is the 'imp', a stone devil that has become the city's emblem. Legend has it that the Devil sent out his imps to do mischief and this one entered the cathedral and ran amok, destroying tapestries and books, so one of the angels from the angel choir turned him to stone. A less fanciful version has it that he was deliberately carved to remind pilgrims to St Hugh's shrine of the dangers of evil. Whichever you go for, imp spotting is a favourite tourist pastime here.

## TENNYSON STATUE (T)

This superb tribute to Lincolnshire's finest poet was designed and sculpted by his friend George Frederick Watts at his Compton studio in Surrey. He had it mounted on rails so he could winch it outside his studio to work on it. It is apparently unfinished and Watts never lived to see it cast in 1903, but it is amongst his finest work. He depicts Tennyson contemplating a flower with his Siberian wolfhound, Karenina, at his side.

## BISHOP'S PALACE (BP)

This is arranged in a series of terraces with what Barley called 'the finest view imaginable'. It was burnt and looted by Royalists in the Civil War and not rebuilt since. The Bishops of Lincoln were some of the most powerful people in England at one time. The west hall and undercroft is particularly fine and Henry VIII was once a guest here. From here we descend Greestone Stairs (GS).

## USHER ART GALLERY (UG)

Built in 1927 and named after James Ward Usher, the city sheriff in 1916. He was a silversmith and he left his exquisite collection of miniatures and watches to the city. The Lincoln Imp was a popular tourist attraction in Victorian times and Usher made a fortune selling replica souvenirs to visitors. The gallery holds many interesting exhibits including some Tennyson memorabilia, but its jewel is a collection of watercolours and sketches by the local artist Peter De Wint. He visited Lincoln in 1806 and later married a Lincoln lass, Harriet Hilton, the sister of the painter William Hilton, which led to him painting many landscapes and rural scenes of Lincoln. He ranks amongst the country's finest watercolourists and his rough field sketches capture vivid snapshots with just a few lines. It is easy to see why he was once credited with coming the nearest of any artist to painting the perfect picture.

## LINCOLN MUSEUM (LM)

Combined with the art gallery, this is now called 'The Collection' and houses imaginative exhibitions relating to many aspects of Lincolnshire history, from Stone Age times through to the Romans, Vikings, Medieval period and beyond. It allows you to delve a little deeper into what you have experienced on this walk.

———————————————————————————————— *Further Reading*

Abell, E. and J. Chambers, *The Story of Lincoln* (The City of Lincoln Education Committee; Lincoln, 1939)

Barley, M.W., *Lincolnshire and the Fens* (Batsford; London, 1952)

Golding, W., *The Spire* (Faber and Faber; London, 1964). This will give you an extraordinary insight into the building of a spire atop a medieval cathedral.

Yates, J. and H. Thorold, *Lincolnshire; A Shell Guide* (Faber and Faber; London, 1965)

www.wattsgallery.org.uk/picture-focus/monument-tennyson

# CARR DYKE

## Along a Roman Canal

Close to Lincoln, this 10-mile walk follows the route of the Roman canal called the Carr Dyke. Little known outside of Lincolnshire and then only to ardent walkers and historians, the dyke deserves a much higher profile, being the second longest Roman monument in Britain after Hadrian's Wall. The history of the dyke is explored, as is the abundant wildlife to be seen on this walk along the edge of the Fens. The route follows the course of the dyke to the village of Martin, where the only refreshments on the route can be found. It then returns via the disused Second World War Metheringham airfield. With two parking points shown on the map, it can easily be broken down into two gentle 5-mile circulars. It is perhaps best done in mid to late summer on a fine sunny day when the butterflies are at their best. At this season it is a Grade 3 walk with easy going most of the way.

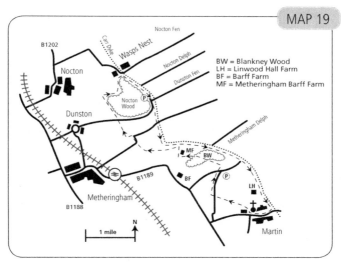

MAP 19

BW = Blankney Wood
LH = Linwood Hall Farm
BF = Barff Farm
MF = Metheringham Barff Farm

The Foss Dyke, connecting the River Witham at Lincoln to the River Trent, and the Carr Dyke are rare examples of Roman canals in Britain. Originally the Carr Dyke would have run from the River Witham just south of Lincoln and connected with the River Nene, 57 miles away near Peterborough. It was thought to be part of an important transport link all the way to York in the north, via the River Ouse. Dr William Stukeley, an eighteenth-century antiquarian who had pioneered the investigation of Stonehenge, suggested that the dyke was used to ferry supplies such as corn up from the Fens to Lincoln and the garrison at York, but the Romans probably also had drainage in mind when they built the canal, and to some extent it still serves this purpose.

More recent archaeology has suggested that its navigability is in doubt and that it may simply have acted as some sort of boundary and drain. Supporting this view is the fact that its route defines the western edge of the Fens. This being so, it is probably best described as a Roman catchwater drain. It was built in sections and water would drain off the high ground to the west and collect in the dyke. From here it was able to flow along the dyke instead of swamping the Fens. You will get a sense of how important this will have been when you get views east across the 'great flatness' that is the Fens; you can see how easily it would have been flooded. As the dyke connects with the rivers Slea, Nene, Welland and Witham it is possible for the water to flow out along these to the sea and so reduce or eliminate the risk.

Much of the dyke has long since disappeared under the plough and development but our stretch represents a well-preserved section.

Along the route are sculptures and benches in oak, reflecting the themes of land reclamation, the Fens and local history.

## WILDLIFE

There is much to be seen along the often tree-lined dyke as it passes through a number of different habitats. Many 'delphs' or drains connect the dyke to the River Witham, helping to drain the adjacent fens for agricultural purposes. These delphs and the dyke, where it is still wet, hold good examples of aquatic vegetation such as reedmace, reed, water dock, water mint and water forget-me-not.

Birds likely to be seen are dependent upon the season and include heron, kingfisher, reed and sedge warblers, alongside waterfowl such as coot, moorhen and mute swans. The dyke is also a good site for the declining turtle dove, whose gentle purring can be heard on a fine sunny day if you are lucky.

Look out, too, for the small-leaved lime, a tree native to Lincolnshire that can be found growing alongside the canal. It has heart-shaped leaves, clusters of 'feathery' flowers and winged seeds. The blossom can be used to make tea that has sedative properties. It was once extensively coppiced and used for fuel and fencing. The wood has a hard grain and is not easily split, so it is favoured by woodcarvers.

## FENS

To your left are a series of fens all the way along this route and it is worth scanning these occasionally to check for barn owls and marsh harriers. In winter, bird numbers are increased by the presence of many duck such as teal, tufted duck, pochard and shovelers and the Fens are then hunted over by both peregrine falcons and the occasional merlin, our smallest bird of prey.

## MARTIN

This village lies on a long straight road over the Fens and is the only refreshment stop on the route. The 1876 Holy Trinity church has some nice grimacing gargoyles in the tower.

The route out of Martin follows the 'stepping out' signposts. These are part of a series of excellent way-marked walks devised by North Kesteven District Council.

## METHERINGHAM AIRFIELD

Metheringham Airfield was home to 106 Lancaster Squadron in the Second World War from 1943. These aircraft were used for bombing raids over Berlin. Over 2,000 people operated the station and sadly fifty-seven Lancasters were lost flying out of here, so take some time to pay your respects at the small memorial here.

You will see the word 'barff' on the map in this area and it is a Lincolnshire term for higher ridges of land running alongside flatter areas such as the Fens. It was an ideal spot for an airfield.

## WASPS NEST

This tiny hamlet is a strong challenger to Mavis Enderby for the best place name in Lincolnshire. Before you drop down into Wasps Nest, look left towards Abbey Hill. This was the site of the twelfth-century Augustinian

# Kids' Stuff

**FIND:**
**A leaved lime.** Check out what this tree looks like beforehand and resolve to find one. A prize to the first to find one and check out www.british-trees.com.

**PLAY:**
**Fen bingo.** Design a bingo card (4x4) for each child with the following written in the squares: a reedmace (bulrush), heron, small leaved-lime, rabbit, carving, yellow iris, yellowhammer, sugar beet factory, stile, any bird of prey, any butterfly, footpath marker, pheasant , tractor, lapwing, lichen. Prizes are awarded for any line of four up, down or diagonally, with a star prize for the full house.

**What is it!** Each person takes a small box or bag on the walk with them and secretly collects six strange objects or things they cannot identify. When home these are exchanged and you each have to identify the others' objects.

**Sound guess!** Whilst walking secretly collect another six things. These could be anything from a feather to a rabbit dropping. When you get home you put the 'thing' into a small container which no one can see through. The others are then allowed to hold the container and they have to guess what's inside from its weight and the sound it makes when they rattle it.

**FIND:**
**Some tree leaves.** Leaves are an excellent way of identifying trees. You will come across a wide variety of trees on this walk so collect leaves from different trees and then when you get home check out which species they are.

priory dedicated to St Mary Magdalene. It was closed in 1536. Coming out of Wasps Nest, the route used to be part of the Nocton Light Railway which operated from 1926 to 1969 and was used for taking sugar beet to the factory at Bardney, which you can see across the fen to the north-east.

## NOCTON WOOD

From Wasps Nest, this bit of Nocton Wood was part of an ancient coppiced woodland and is a good spot for birds, so keep an eye out for treecreepers and long-tailed tits which are commonly seen here.

——————————————————————————————— *Further Reading*

Simmons, B. and P. Cope-Faulkner, *The Carr Dyke* (Heritage Lincolnshire; Heckington, 2006). This is a fascinating and very readable account of the dyke, discussing its building and purpose and is based upon hours of local fieldwork and expertise. Archaeology at its best.
www.metheringhamairfield.com
www.countrysidenk.co.uk

# A WOODLAND CINEMA AND IMPRESSIVE FLYPASTS

Woodhall Spa to Tattershall

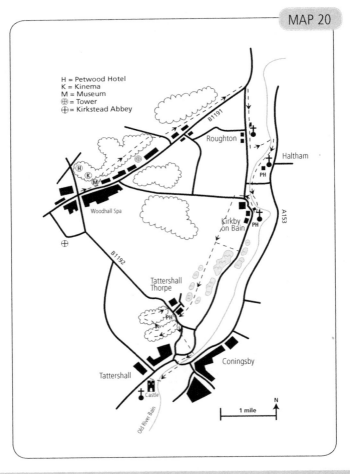

MAP 20

H = Petwood Hotel
K = Kinema
M = Museum
⊕ = Tower
⊕ = Kirkstead Abbey

B1191

Roughton

Haltham

PH

Woodhall Spa

Kirkby on Bain

PH

A153

B1192

Tattershall Thorpe

PH

Coningsby

Tattershall

Castle

Old River Bain

1 mile

N

This is a varied 12-mile walk with just about a bit of everything in it. We begin at the 'inland resort' of Woodhall Spa and explore its secrets before heading north-east along the disused Woodhall to Horncastle railway line and Viking Way. The route then heads south along the valley of the River Bain through Roughton and along the disused Horncastle Canal to Haltham and Kirkby on Bain, before continuing south to Tattershall Thorpe. Here is a wonderful 'Military Camp' museum for some unashamed 1940s nostalgia and reminders of the huge part this area played in the Second World War. From here we explore Tattershall Thorpe woods and head on into Tattershall, where we encounter Tom Thumb and a medieval castle. It is possible to park in Tattershall and get a bus or alternatively park at either end and get a taxi to the other to start the walk. You can also explore Tattershall and Woodhall separately as two shorter walks. The full walk is Grade 5 because of its length, but the going is easy.

## WOODHALL SPA

The spa element begins with one John Parkinson who wanted to found a city, plant a forest and dig a mine hereabouts. There is a 'Coal Pit Wood' here and the town sign still has a coal pit wheel on it too. Parkinson succeeded in planting many fir and oak trees, but the mining venture thankfully failed. At a depth of around 540 feet the mineshaft flooded and in 1827 he went bankrupt.

However, the clear salty water was found to have curative properties. Ailing cattle were seen to benefit from it first and eventually people began to try it out on their ills and the spa town grew up on the basis of this. The waters, containing iodine and bromine, were said to help sufferers of gout and rheumatism in particular. The spa began with a pump room and bathhouse built over the shaft and several large and very grand hotels were built. A stay here 'taking the waters' would have been a very pleasant experience, situated as it was amongst sandy heathlands surrounded by birch trees, bracken and, more recently, rhododendrons. The spa was very popular and there was much expansion from 1855, with thousands of visitors taking advantage of the new railways to come and visit what was described as an 'inland resort'. The pump room in the pine woods next to the 'Kinema' can still be seen, but sadly it is derelict and rather unsightly now.

# DAMBUSTERS

In 1943 the Petwood Hotel became the officers' mess of the 617 'Dambusters' squadron led by Wing Commander Guy Gibson and the squadron bar contains memorabilia relating to this. You must return here after the walk and drink a toast as the bar has a real sense of history. Gibson was awarded the Victoria Cross for his efforts, only to go missing in action on a raid in 1944 at the age of 25.

In Woodhall you will find a memorial, built in the shape of a dam, to the many airman from across the globe who gave their lives for the freedom of others. The raid on the Ruhr dams, called Operation Chastise, was carried out on 16/17 May 1943 by Lancaster bombers taking off from RAF Scampton. The raid was of huge significance and its heroism and daring captured the imagination of all. It used Barnes Wallis' bouncing bombs to inflict severe damage on industry in the Ruhr valley by breaching two of the dams. However, eight Lancasters and fifty-three aircrew were lost. It is said that occasionally the sound of the dambusters' crew drinking can be heard in the squadron bar!

The nearby Lincolnshire Aviation Heritage centre at East Kirkby houses a still-taxiing Lancaster; if you have never heard the sound of its Merlin engines being fired up then a visit here is a must for another day.

# KINEMA IN THE WOODS

Locally referred to as the 'Flicks in the Sticks', you should try to coincide your walk with an evening here as a cinema finale.

The Kinema started life as a sports pavilion in the grounds of the Victoria Hotel, one of the key spa hotels. This burnt down in 1920 and the pavilion was converted into a cinema in 1922. The first film shown was one of Charlie Chaplin's and the Kinema is the only one in the UK using a rare form of rear projection from behind the screen. In its heyday the first six rows were deckchairs, but they were cheaper and so highly sought after. On selected performances you can also hear the original Compton organ, which still rises from the floor before the film.

Also well worth a visit is the Woodhall Cottage Museum, which houses much memorabilia about the town and its spa days.

# KIRKSTEAD ABBEY

If time permits, take a walk out to see this romantic ruin. Founded in 1139, but not completed until around 1187, it was originally populated by monks

from Fountains Abbey in Yorkshire. It is one of several Cistercian abbeys in this part of Lincolnshire, alongside Bardney, Revesby, Stainfield, Barlings and Tupholme, all of them seeking seclusion. What is left is a picturesque ruined tower which one cannot but get the urge to climb. Looking at the surrounding earthworks and the remnants of the moat, you get some idea of the size the abbey complex used to be.

After the abbey was dissolved in 1537, the last abbott and three monks were executed for their part in the Lincolnshire Uprising. The monks built a chapel just outside the abbey and this is still in existence. This Chapel of St Leonard has some nice dog-toothed arches and a fine west front and doorway. Inside, vaulting reaches up to large bosses including a superb 'Lamb of God'. There is also some richly carved foliage, especially on the lancet windows at the east end, a tribute to the stonemason's craft.

Leaving Woodhall along the Viking Way, past the golf links, is the brick 'Tower on the Moor' on your right, attributed to the Cromwells of Tattershall.

## ROUGHTON

Here we find an elegant eighteenth-century hall and St Margaret's church, which is a nice jumbled patchwork of greenstone, red brick and limestone from practically every century since it was built. Apparently bits were added whenever a particularly good harvest released sufficient cash! It dates from the thirteenth century and has the base of a medieval cross in the churchyard. Inside you can see some thirteenth-century windows, a twelfth-century font and a panelled pulpit with 'barley twist balusters and an Ionic fluted knopped newel'.

Leaving Roughton we follow the Horncastle Canal which was opened in 1802 for taking grain and malt out of Horncastle, and coal and timber in. It had eleven locks in 11 miles and its last barge sailed through in 1878, carrying 31 tons of guano from Boston to Horncastle. This was used as a fertiliser, but where on earth did they get it? Today the canal is a great asset to the wildlife of the area, with kingfishers often spotted.

## HALTHAM

It is worth a quick detour into the village here. The Marmion Arms was named after the family of the original King's Champion, Robert Marmion. He was granted this right and the manor of nearby Scrivelsby by William the Conqueror in 1066. St Benedict's church is being restored and has a huge east window with beautiful stone tracery and there are medieval pews, and a three-decker pulpit. One of the family box pews belonged to the Dymokes of Scrivelsby, who took over from the Marmions as King's Champion. There is also what might be a Knights Templar cross, carved above the Norman door, and a beautiful face carved into an arch base. In fact, there are superb carved faces to be found all over this church.

The Ebrington Arms, built in 1610, retains much of its original character, with tree trunk beams, mud and stud walls. In one beam you can see the old coins that airmen and soldiers pushed into the beams as prepayment for a beer on their return from missions.

## KIRKBY ON BAIN

According to Thorold and Yates, this is a long 'undistinguished' village. See what you think. The name Kirkby derives from the Danish for church, hence 'kirk' in Scotland. St Mary's church has three windows in the east end by William Morris & Co. Also check out the grave of Thomas Would, who died in 1799 aged 31, whose headstone reads:

Farwel, vain World; Ive had enough of thee.
And am carlefs of what thou sayst of me;
Thy smiles I count not nor they frowns I fear,
My care is past my Head lays quiet here
What faults thou sawest in me be sure to 'XXXXX'
And look at home. Enough is to be done

Can you decipher the missing word?

The path now takes us past a municipal rubbish tip and across a boardwalk that goes over a series of gravel workings on its way to Tattershall Thorpe. Winter turns these pits into a refuge for an impressive range of wildfowl.

## TATTERSHALL THORPE

The Bluebell has been an inn since the sixteenth century, when it lay on a drover's road. It is built of mud and stud and houses some memorabilia relating to the airmen from RAF Woodhall Spa. It boasts some signatures of members of the 617 squadron on its ceiling.

## THORPE CAMP VISITOR CENTRE

This is an excellent museum sited in the old NAAFI, airmen's dining halls and ration stores. There are good reconstructions of military scenes and rooms, a bomb-damaged room, Anderson shelter, prisoner of war display, a wartime kitchen and much more. There are also occasionally some 1940s reconstruction days, inclusive of live '40s music shows. These are excellent and really do bring the past to life, so try and coincide you walk with one of these and do the walk wearing 1940s hiking gear!

## CARR WOODS

The woods here are important ancient woodlands under the protection of the Woodland Trust. At one time they were regularly coppiced. Look out for alders and hazels with their catkins and willows in the wetter areas. Keep an ear out in spring for the drumming of great spotted and green woodpeckers. Spring also brings marvellous displays of snowdrops, followed by primroses, bluebells and wood sorrel. A dawn or dusk visit may well bring you a sighting of woodcock roding and throughout the day, especially in spring when ground cover is good, you have the chance to see and hear muncjac and roe deer. In the Carr Wood you will also notice the remains of wartime bunkers and bomb shelters.

The next feature of note as we head towards Tattershall is the disused railway. This was part of the Lincoln–Boston line, which is sadly missed. It took about 1½ hours on the train, which was great improvement on the 6 hours that the steam boat along the River Witham used to take, before trade ended in 1860.

## TATTERSHALL

The market square has a fifteenth-century buttercross bearing Ralph Cromwell's coat of arms. It hosted a market from 1201 and the annual Tattershall Fair, though sadly they are no longer. The Fortescue Arms dates from the eighteenth century, having once been a coaching inn, but the main interest in the square is Tom Thumb's house sitting atop a ridge tile. It is said to be a device to help ward off evil spirits, having no connection with the actual Tom Thumb!

## TATTERSHALL CASTLE

This magnificent keep is one of the finest medieval brick buildings in England. It is a superb, solid, six-storey construction, at 110 feet high with walls 20 feet thick at the base. It was built from over a million bricks made at Edlington Moor, just north of Woodhall. The first castle on this site was built by Robert de Tateshale in around 1230 and Ralph Cromwell began work on what now remains in 1433. Cromwell had fought alongside

# Kids' Stuff

**TRY:**
**Some Lincolnshire words.** Why don't they make languages this interesting at school? There is a certain pleasure in accusing someone of something they can't understand, so don't let me catch you …

Stiving – sneaking about

Brogging – interfering with things (poking about)

Gizzening – wandering about aimlessly

Stithering – going on and on and on about something

**PLAY:**
**Autumn woodland bingo.** Design a bingo card (4x4) for each child with these things written in the squares: rhododendron, birch, bramble, acorn, elderberry, hawthorn berry, ivy berry, hazel nuts, conkers, a toadstool, a bracket fungus, an old bird's nest, deer hoof marks, a leaf skeleton, squirrel, a spider's web, insect galls, a winged seed, a pine cone, woodpigeon.

**MAKE:**
**Some woodland floor art.** As you walk through the woods gather as many different kinds of things as possible: big leaves, twigs, feathers, conkers, etc. Then, at a suitable spot, arrange them into a huge pattern on the woodland floor. Try circles or stars but make them as big and bold as possible. Then leave them as a surprise piece of art for the next wood walkers.

**A leaf chart.** Collect as many different kinds of leaf as possible and then, when you get home, try and identify them all. Then dry them and press them in an old book and make your own wall chart by sticking them down and labelling them.

**A goblin's house!** When in the woods, make a frame from twigs like a wigwam and cover it with ferns and other leaves. Put some leaves and moss on the floor as a carpet and try and make it as cosy as possible. Others who come across it will be very curious to know what it is and who made it. Maybe a small animal will come across it and use it as its shelter.

**LOOK UP:**
Medieval castle latrines

Tom Thumb

Bouncing bombs. Find out how the Lancaster bombers managed to fly at a steady 60 feet, the optimum height for getting the most out of their bouncing bombs

Henry V at Agincourt and was said to be the power behind the throne, being Lord High Treasurer of England to Henry VI. This was the medieval equivalent of Chancellor of the Exchequer and his emblem was a purse. He had many other impressive titles but was allegedly also very unpopular. His castle was not built for defence but as a home and it is rather an ostentatious status symbol; lucky man.

The castle underwent reconstruction from 1912–14 by Lord Curzon of Keddleston, who eventually bequeathed it to the National Trust. It has four floors each with a central hall and containing some magnificently ornate chimney pieces which bear the coats of arms of many families associated with the Cromwells. Look out for the carvings of the treasurer's purse, Cromwell's symbol.

All floors are connected by a stone spiral staircase with a countersunk stone handrail in the south-east corner turret. The National Trust guidebook has some interesting images of how the castle might once have looked and worked. It tells us, for example, that the latrines were basically shafts in the walls which discharged into the moat (strictly no swimming) and were open at the top for ventilation.

From the roof of the castle there is a wide panorama and you can see both Boston Stump and Lincoln Cathedral, which are 32 miles from each other. And as Peach points out, if you look very hard you can also see New York, a village about 4 miles away!

## THE BEDE HOUSES AND COLLEGIATE CHURCH

Apart from making his home in the castle, Cromwell also founded a college and school, the remains of which are behind some houses in the market square and in the care of English Heritage. The composer John Tavener was allegedly one of its pupils. In 1440 he also founded the almshouses or Bede cottages, which housed thirteen old and needy locals who had to wear a uniform of rough, russet coloured cloth – look for a carved stone head in the west end gable. Not content with this, he also oversaw the building of the collegiate church. Holy Trinity church was founded in 1439 and is a huge perpendicular church with over sixty windows through which pours the pure Lincolnshire light.

It has lost its medieval stained glass as in 1737 the vicar, Samuel Kirkshawe, complained that he couldn't see to read his sermons. This took seventeen years to resolve and in 1754 the glass was sold to the Earl of Exeter and taken to Stamford. This was nearly the cause of a Tattershall uprising, as it angered the locals, but the glass was snatched in the middle of the night a day before a demonstration against its sale was planned. Following this the church remained glassless for fifty years, causing much internal damage such as rotted pews, not to mention many colds amongst the congregation. Yates and Thorold describe the inside as a 'grand, threadbare interior'. It is the long 60-foot chancel which gives the church its airiness, but it is still a magnificent interior with brasses to the Cromwell dynasty, a carved wooden pulpit and a fine stone screen. Look for Cromwell's purse symbol carved into the lower part of the pulpit and also in one of the windows.

There is also a burial slab to Tom Thumb as legend has it that he was buried here. It tells us that he died in 1620, aged 101. The church also has a thriving colony of Pipistrelle and Daubenton bats.

## CONNINGSBY

St Michael's parish church has a large clock face (16½ feet across) painted in white on its tower. It only has an hour hand, but this is so big that you can quite accurately tell the time, the intention being that it could be read from a way off in the Fens. The clock's red centre and blue outer ring link the church with the RAF base here and the church contains RAF memorabilia. The airfield was the base for mosquito pathfinder squadrons and the dambusters. Today it is home to Tornado and Typhoon fighter planes, which you may hear and see, usually in that order. It is also home to the Battle of Britain Memorial Flight, so if you're lucky you might also get to see Lancasters and Spitfires flying past.

Baldwin, M., 'A Miscellany of Old Lincolnshire' in *Lincolnshire Life* (Dec 1966, Vol. 6, No. 10, P31)

'Tattershall Castle' (National Trust, 1997)

Peach, H., *Lincolnshire Curiosities* (The Dovecote Press; Wimborne, 1994)

Yates, J. and H. Thorold, *Lincolnshire; A Shell Guide* (Faber and Faber; London, 1965)

www.thorpecamp.org.uk

www.lincsaviation.co.uk

www.bbmf.co.uk

www.tattershallwiththorpe.co.uk

www.britishlistedbuildings.co.uk

www.thekinemainthewoods.co.uk

# THE ANCASTER GAP WALK

This 11-mile walk begins by boarding the Sleaford-bound train at Ancaster and getting off at the next stop, Rauceby, approximately 6 minutes later! The walk begins and ends at Lincolnshire Wildlife Trust nature reserves

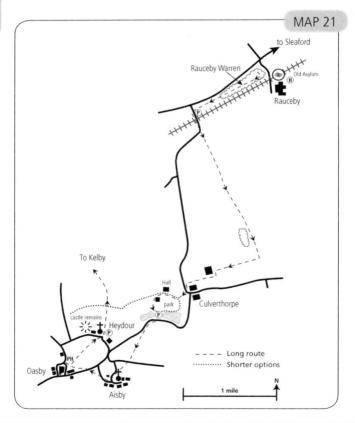

MAP 21

to Sleaford

Rauceby Warren

Old Asylum

Rauceby

To Kelby

Hall

park

Culverthorpe

castle remains

Heydour

PH

Oasby

Aisby

– – – Long route
· · · · · · · · Shorter options

1 mile

N

MAP 22

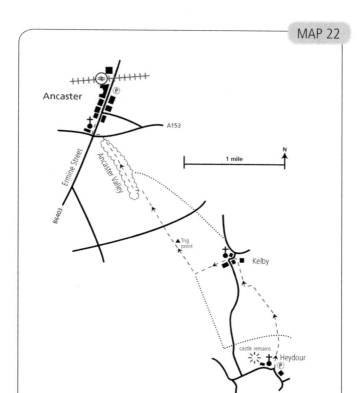

Raceby Warren and Ancaster Valley. Between the two, it takes in Culverthorpe with its lake and hall, then the small triangle of villages Aisby, Oasby and Heydour before returning to Ancaster via Kelby. Several shorter options are available, such as a 6-mile figure of eight taking in five villages and an even shorter 3-mile circuit, which misses out Kelby, and an even shorter mile-long circuit around Culverthorpe Lake and Hall. Alternatively you can park on Ancaster's broad Ermine Street or at the playing fields car park and walk to Kelby and back via Ancaster Valley. The paths can get very muddy in autumn and winter, so it can be a long day out. A Grade 2 walk in dry weather, but a 4 in the wet.

## RAUCEBY STATION

This is the station serving the villages of North and South Rauceby, 1½ miles north of here, over the A153. The only other benefactor of the station is the old Rauceby Hospital or Kesteven County Asylum, as it was called when it opened in 1902. During the 1940s it became a RAF crash and burns unit called the Guinea Pig Club, where plastic surgeons such as Archibald McIndoe undertook pioneering experimental reconstructive plastic surgery. The hospital remains are now buried in a modern housing estate, so the walk heads straight out by the A153 and into Rauceby Warren.

## RAUCEBY WARREN

This is a once-sandy warren turned heathland, but later worked for sand and gravel and thus is now a series of pits which vary between being full of water and dried out, according to the seasonal conditions. There is flora here reminiscent of the Breckland of Norfolk and it is home to a national rarity called smooth rupturewort, which is an inconspicuous mat-forming green herb which, liking poor soils, used to grow in the car park. Look out too for viper's bugloss and, in summer, the many species of butterfly that thrive here, and check the stone walls for common lizards on warm days. The walk leaves the warren and heads south along a fine track towards Culverthorpe.

## CULVERTHORPE

Culverthorpe Hall is a stone mansion set in parkland overlooking its lake. It was built by Sir John Newton around 1680 but the Palladian wings are a later eighteenth-century addition with older stable buildings on either side. There are superb horse chestnuts along the main drive and a fine walk around the lake.

From Culverthorpe we head south-west to Aisby and its large village green, before turning west to Oasby.

## OASBY

There is no church in the village but note the Houblon Arms. Culverthorpe Hall passed to this family after the Newtons, hence the pub's name. A certain Sir John Houblon was the first Governor of the Bank of England. You may have seen him as his portrait is on the back of older £50 notes. A short hop across the fields brings you to Heydour.

## HEYDOUR

St Michael's church has a 'lofty' spire with 'big' pinnacles, according to Yates and Thorold, and there is some superb medieval glass depicting various saints, angels and knights. There is also a side chapel behind the organ, containing many monuments to the Newton family, who were relatives of Sir Isaac. They are especially poignant and superbly carved. One wall tablet is from Lady Frances Coningsby, dedicated to her sister Margaret 'Countefs' of Coningsby and tells of how they were 'Kindred and concordant hearts' and her unutterable grief. There is also one to the infant viscount, Margaret's son, who was apparently dropped over the parapet of their house in 1733 by the family pet monkey!

West of the church is a nineteenth-century farmhouse with a strange figure over the porch. At one time Heydour had a castle or fortified Norman manor house and a little further up the road one can make out some traces of its ringworks in the field. From Heydour we head north from the church, past the old schoolhouse, towards Kelby.

## KELBY

St Andrew's church has an embattled west tower and spire with some wonderful grotesque faces staring at you.

Inside it has a fine decorated south aisle with a good vaulted roof. Check out the old poppy heads in the nave.

## ANCASTER VALLEY

We approach the valley along what is a glorious golden tree tunnel in the autumn. A bridleway signpost then points you down a short flight of steps into the valley. According to some sources, the Romans used this valley for chariot racing. This has never been proven but what a fantastic thought. This is now a superb place for limestone-loving flowers, including bee orchids, and one could easily spend a day here botanising. The valley side holds a wide range of trees and shrubs, some of which are seldom seen. Sheep graze the reserve to preserve the grass by preventing scrubland encroaching and then woodland forming. In the autumn this is a superb place to brush up on your berry and seed identification and in summer is a fine place to test your butterfly recognition skills.

# ANCASTER

There was a Roman station or fort here which developed into the town called Causennae, and much 'Romanalia' has been unearthed hereabouts. Finds include thousands of coins and a sculpture called *Deae Matres*, depicting three pregnant Mother-Goddesses holding food. This was a fertility symbol for the Romans. It was found in the churchyard in 1831 and is now in Grantham museum, but a replica of it sits on the church wall.

It is no surprise to find that the Roman road Ermine Street passes right through the middle of the village. The settlement is sited at a gap in the limestone ridge which forms Lincolnshire's backbone and was likely cut by an Ice Age tributary of the River Trent. Before the Romans, Stone Age man resided in the gap and just down the road at Honington was the main Iron Age camp in Lincolnshire.

The village is famous for its hardwearing limestone, which was used in the House of Commons and St Pancras station and more locally in Belton House and Lincoln Cathedral. The broad main street is described by Yates and Thorold as having a certain 'grim attractiveness', which is the best example of sitting on the fence I have come across in a while.

St Martin's church has a Norman nave arcade with some nicely decorated Norman arches, Norman style font decorated with lovely intertwined arches and some nice wall tablets to the Lucas-Calcraft family. Outside are some very interesting and photogenic gravestones made from Ancaster stone. The local masons developed a certain style of monument fashioned by the properties of the stone. It is a large slab tapered towards the foot and supported by two vertical slabs holding it about a foot off the ground.

# Kids' Stuff

**DRAW:**
**The best poppy head.** Kelby church is the venue and there are plenty of poppy heads to choose from. The winner gets a bunch of flowers for their bedroom. Parents must not judge this: find a friendly local and ask them to invigilate!

**PHOTOGRAPH:**
**The best Ancaster gravestone.** This should not only be judged on being a technically perfect photo, but also on its history or unusualness.

**FIND:**
**Berries and seeds.** In autumn this is a great place for finding lots of different berries and seeds. So take a small box and collect as many different kinds as possible and look them up when you get home. Alternatively, photograph them, as it often helps to know the leaf shape too.

**The smooth rupturewort.** Check out what this looks like online and, armed with some pictures, carefully examine the ground for signs of it at Rauceby Warren.

**MAKE:**
**Bramble tarts.** If you do this walk around autumn take a plastic box and collect some brambles. You will have to research how to make jam, but essentially you boil the fruit with water and sugar and add some pectin to make it set. Next make your pastry and add your jam and bake them. Cut thin strips of pastry and put people's initials on the top of the tarts.

**Leaf art!** Gather as many different kinds of leaf as you can throughout the day, then when you get home make a picture or collage from them.

**WATCH:**
**The butterflies.** Get hold of a good small butterfly identification chart or book (try www.naturedetyectioves.org.uk) and check each butterfly you see and keep a list of them. You will be amazed how many you can see in summer on this walk.

The overflow cemetery (out of the back of the churchyard and turn right), is a Site of Special Scientific Interest and one of only two places in the country where tall thrift grows. Note also the (now open) stone coffins from the Roman cemetery which was sited here.

*Further Reading*

Yates, J. and H. Thorold, *Lincolnshire; A Shell Guide* (Faber and Faber; London, 1965)
www.raucebyhospital.8m.com/index.html
www.en.wikipedia.org/wiki/Guinea_Pig_Club

# STAMFORD AND ITS VILLAGES

Beginning and ending in Stamford, this 14-mile route explores beautiful stone-built villages and parkland, and there are also some fine churches and pubs to explore along the way. It passes through the grounds of Casewick Hall and in Greatford there are strange stone sculptures to explore. The area is rich in local history, boasting a spa resort at Braceborough and strong connections with early psychiatric care, in particular Dr Francis Willis who

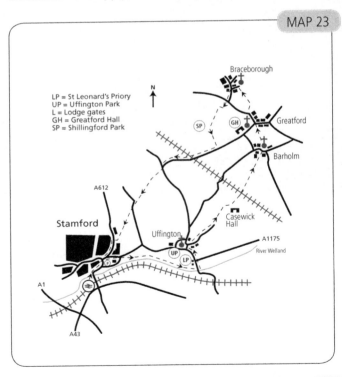

MAP 23

LP = St Leonard's Priory
UP = Uffington Park
L = Lodge gates
GH = Greatford Hall
SP = Shillingford Park

'cured' the madness of King George III. There is an abundance of wildlife to be seen along the way and the walk ends with an exploration of the fine town of Stamford, which H.D. Martineau called a 'Symphony in Stone'. It will probably take you two days, one for Stamford and one for the walk, but what better place for an overnight stay? There is plenty of parking in Stamford and the walk is on good paths, but it is Grade 4 due to length.

Start the walk down by the meadows and go across them to George Bridge to get a view of the town and its spires. Then walk down Bath Row to Wharf Road and Priory Road.

## ST LEONARD'S PRIORY (LP)

This is a lovely ruin, the church founded around 1100 by Benedictine monks from Durham. All that remains are bits of the priory church comprising the nave, the Norman west front and some arches of the north arcade.

From here, after the roundabout and garage, we turn right down towards the river. Take good care not to disturb the crocodile by the weir and keep to the path north of the river. You might catch a glimpse of the turrets of

Burghley House to the right as you cross this field towards the remains of the Stamford or Welland Navigation Canal. This used to link Stamford to the East Coast from 1673 to 1863 until the coming of the railways.

This is a good spot to see Goatsbeard or 'Jack-go-to-bed-at-noon', so named because its large dandelion-like flowers close up at midday. Children will love seeing the large seed heads. The canal and river meet a narrow stone bridge and just up the road towards Uffington there are some splendid gates by the two stone lodges at the entrance to Uffington Park. Notice the strange surprised crowned figures sitting atop the gate posts!

## UFFINGTON

This lovely stone-built village harbours the church of St Michael and All Angels, with its crocketed spire.

It also boasts Ye Olde Bertie Arms, a thatched inn dating back to 1681 and named after the local lords of the manor, the Bertie family (the Earls of Lindsey). The Berties moved here in 1670 but the house was destroyed by fire in 1904. Opposite the church is a late seventeenth-century garden gate for Uffington Park and the little of what remains of the formal gardens.

The village also has a stone lion's head fountain, erected in 1897 for Queen Victoria's diamond jubilee, and the churchyard holds some beautiful gravestones. The church also has some fine monuments, including the tomb of a knight said to be Richard de Schropshire and one to the Manners brothers, Oliver and Roger. And don't miss the window depicting Faith, Hope and Charity. The crowning glory of the church, however, is the quality of the stone carving inside. Check out the font, the pulpit canopy and most of all the fantastic corbels, each depicting a separate scene such as Adam and Eve being expelled from the Garden of Eden and Abraham about to kill Isaac.

## CASEWICK HALL

We next walk towards Casewick Park and along its main drive, right past the hall. This was a medieval country house remodelled in the early seventeenth century by the Trollope family. It is a mix of Gothic and Jacobean, with its mullioned windows and stepped gables. The hall has many ancillary buildings including a coach house, granary, stables, brew house, dairy and kitchen. Beyond the hall, take care crossing the main-line railway on your way to Barholm as super-fast express trains thunder by on a regular basis.

## BARHOLM

Here are more fine stone houses, an old hall and an early English and Norman church. The tower was rebuilt in 1648 in the Civil War and is inscribed:

Was ever such a thing
Since the Creation?
A newe steeple built
In the time of vexation

Less vexing is the seventeenth-century real ale pub, the Five Horseshoes!

## GREATFORD

With the West Glen River flowing through it, this stone village has changed little in the last 100 years. The thirteenth-century church of St Thomas Becket has a broach spire described by Barley as a 'very graceful achievement of the thirteenth century mason'. In the North Transept there is a memorial to Dr Francis Willis, who is buried here. The memorial refers to his curing King George III of his madness. It tells of how he pursued 'the bent of his natural taste and inclination' to become a physician and was 'the chief agent in removing the malady which afflicted the present majesty in the year 1789.'

Willis ran a private asylum here in Greatford Hall. The sixteenth-century hall burnt down in 1922 and was reconstructed and can just be seen from the roadside.

Greatford's other claim to fame is its strange stone carvings, such as the sofa outside the Hare & Hounds, large crowns in gardens, naked maidens, ornamental bowls, toadstools, and elephants to cite just a few!

It's worthwhile having a quick wander around the village to see which ones you can spot.

These were designed and made in the 1930s by Major C.C.L. FitzWilliams, who used to live at Greatford Hall. They were to advertise his landscape artist qualities – everyone needs a hobby.

## BRACEBOROUGH

Braceborough was an attempt at a nineteenth-century spa town, with spa house, a small hotel and a railway station. Mineral waters still flow, but this was about a mile north-west of the village. Look for Spa House on the map. According to Yates and Thorold, this 'ill-fated' spa gave up 1.5 million gallons of its 'special' water a day and George III is said to have 'taken the waters' when he was being treated by Francis Willis.

The village hall used to be the school and was built by the Willis family in 1870. The church of St Margaret, dating back to the fourteenth century, has some good stained glass and old gravestones dating back to the seventeenth century. Also notice the figure sticking its tongue out at you as you enter!

From here the walk heads back south to Stamford via Shillingthorpe Park, where another of Dr Willis' asylums, Shillingthorpe Hall, once stood.

## STAMFORD

The town is almost equidistant between the Humber and London and lies at a strategic point on a prehistoric route, the Jurassic Ridgeway, where the River Welland can be crossed. The town derives its name from this stoney ford. The Welland was navigable to the Wash for hundreds of years, snaking its way through the Fens, and it was thus an important contributor to Stamford's early importance for the Danes and Saxons.

It lost out to Lincoln in the ninth and tenth centuries, when the counties were divided and named, otherwise we would be walking in Stamfordshire. Moving on to just after the Norman conquests, William the Conqueror built a castle here which, as it wasn't needed for defensive purposes, eventually fell into decay. Now only a part of the curtain wall survives.

By the late thirteenth century, Stamford was a great trading centre with a big wool trade and a cloth-dominated fair, attracting merchants from Europe. In this era most of the cloth for the royal households was bought at Lincolnshire fairs. The wool trade declined from the fourteenth century, but Stamford remained a prosperous town and in the Middle Ages it had fifteen churches and six priories. St Leonard's Priory was established at around 1100 (actually built upon the site of the monastery founded by St Wilfrid in 658) and all four orders (Franciscans, Dominicans, Carmelites and Austins) eventually had a presence in Stamford. Thus the town became an important religious centre and in the 1330s there was an attempt to establish a university here.

The good times, however, had to end and Henry VIII's Dissolution of the Monasteries closed the town monasteries and several of its churches, thus reducing the town's importance.

Cromwell visited Stamford in the civil war, commandeering Burghley House and destroying the Eleanor Cross. At the end of the Civil War, Charles I is said to have spent his last night of freedom here before riding to Southwell, where he was betrayed to Parliamentary forces.

In the seventeenth and eighteenth century, the local, warm-tinted limestone and some gifted architecture helped to give Stamford an elegance lacking in other towns, with Georgian houses almost everywhere you look. In fact there are over 600 Grade II listed buildings within the old town. Stamford became a great coaching town lying on the Great North Road and by 1830 forty mail coaches and thirty stagecoaches passed through Stamford each day. The best preserved coaching inn is the George (TG).

As you walk in, the room on the left is marked London for those travelling south, and on the right is a room marked York. The famous gallows across the street outside, proclaiming the hotel's name, were erected as a welcome to the honest traveller and a warning to slow down as you come over the hill if you didn't want to end up in the river. They also served as a warning to highwaymen, but they were never meant to be used in anger. The year 1846 saw the coming of the railways to Stamford, amid fears that it would put an end to the coaching trade. However, we should be grateful that the main line went through Peterborough and not Stamford, as this has probably saved the town from much industrial development. It is hard to believe today, as you wander about the streets, that the Great North Road that we call the A1 ran right through the centre until 1960, when a bypass was opened.

Our suggested route through the town takes in the following buildings in this order.


## BROWNE'S HOSPITAL (BH)

In 1475 a rich wool merchant, William Browne, built the hospital of All Saints in Broad Street. These were medieval almshouses, originally for ten men and two women. The current cottages are from 1870 and built around a courtyard, but the inhabitants originally lived in the common room, which was divided into cubicles. There is a large chapel with stalls and misericords and some fine medieval stained glass. In the same street the cruel sport of bull running took place until 1839.


## ALL SAINTS CHURCH (AS)

Browne, together with his brother John, also restored All Saints church and the church has brasses to the Browne family, including a life-size one of William and his wife in the South Chapel. The church dates from the thirteenth century and also has some good Victorian stained glass, alongside multiple arched wall arcading and a semi-detached tower and spire. Be sure to note the carved winged creatures on the ends of the

MAP 24

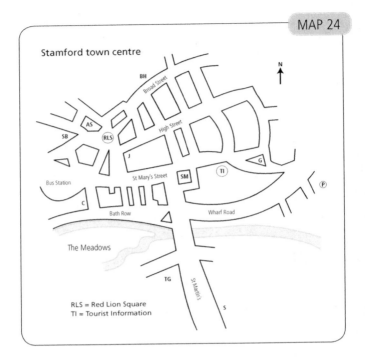

Stamford town centre

RLS = Red Lion Square
TI = Tourist Information

chancel benches. Dr William Stukeley, the forerunner of archaeology and friend of Isaac Newton, was the vicar here from 1730 to 1747.

## STAMFORD STEAM BREWERY (SB)

This is a steam-operated Victorian brewery, no longer working, alas. However, it still houses all the original nineteenth-century equipment.

## ST JOHN THE BAPTIST CHURCH (J)

This is a fifteenth-century perpendicular church, whose carved roof has some interesting carvings of angels, one of whom is ringing handbells. Also look at the carved corbels of grotesque faces and the poppy head bench ends.

## CASTLE REMAINS (C)

The three remaining arches are on the corner of Castle Dyke.

# Kids' Stuff

For younger children, as well as visiting the town you could get a taxi to Braceborough and walk back to Stamford via our outward route.

## TRY:

**Magnifying things!** Take a large magnifying glass on the walk with you and get a look at things from very close up. Try it out on insects, flowers and inside churches. Look at lichens on gravestones and inspect the fine details of carvings, paintings or ornaments.

## MAKE:

**An ice hanging.** When out on a walk, make a small collection such as a feather or two, a nicely shaped twig, a few flowers and an acorn maybe. Then when you get home, place them in a shallow dish and fill with water. Place a loop of string in the dish with the ends hanging out and place in the freezer overnight. In the morning, take it outside and hang it up and enjoy you artwork before it melts. It works well using a plate too, as this gives you a thin shiny disc, but it will not last long in the sun.

## PLAY:

**An alphabet hunt.** Before the walk give everybody a sheet with the alphabet on it down the left-hand side. Throughout the walk, people shout out as you see something beginning with that letter. Only the person who shouts it first can record it; the others have to spy something else starting with that letter.

## LOOK UP:
Perpendicular
Broach spire
Eleanor Cross

## ST MARY'S CHURCH (SM)

This church has a beautiful thirteenth-century tower and fourteenth-century broach spire. Yates and Thorold describe the interior as 'rich and luminous' and be sure to notice the beautiful modern Shepherd Window. Outside, check the nineteenth-century shop fronts in St Mary's Hill and Street, and look for the Norman arch opposite St Mary's.

## ST GEORGE'S CHURCH (G)

This church was built in 1449 by William de Bruges, the first Garter King of Arms. It has a chancel window which incorporates the mottoes of founder members of the Order of the Garter.

## ST MARTIN'S CHURCH (S)

Built around 1430 and perpendicular, this church lies just across the River Welland. This used to be in Northamptonshire until the boundaries changed in 1889, and houses the first Lord Burghley's Renaissance tomb.

It also has the medieval window glass taken from Holy Trinity church in Tattershall, much to the congregation's annoyance. It looks a bit like a patchwork quilt made of odds and ends. In the farther churchyard you will find Daniel Lambert's grave, known as the heaviest man in England. He was only 5 feet tall, but his body was 9 feet 4 inches in circumference (i.e. a 112-inch waist) and he weighed in at 52 stone and 11 pounds. His walking stick is in the George, alongside a portrait. Born in Leicester, he apparently ate little and drank only water, and was passing through Stamford when he died suddenly in the Waggon & Horses, aged 39. The story has it that the window and a wall of the pub had to be knocked down to get his coffin out!

## BURGHLEY HOUSE

This is not on our walk, but we can't talk of Stamford without paying it due homage, and it would be well worth staying an extra day to visit it. The Cecil family rose to prominence in the sixteenth century with William Cecil, Lord Burghley, being the Secretary of State for Queen Elizabeth I, and she granted him the manor of Burghley. Started in 1555, the building took over thirty-two years to complete. It was extensively altered in the seventeenth century by the 5th Earl of Exeter, who established the fine art collection. There are state rooms and fine porcelain and furniture, tapestries and superb Grinling Gibbons wood carvings. The Heaven room, painted by Verrio, is said to be the finest painted room in England, with nymphs, satyrs, goddesses and cherubs tumbling from the ceiling into the room, complete with rainbow. Then, by complete contrast, there is the Hell staircase, also painted by Verrio, depicting death, torment and despair in the most disturbing detail. It is staggering. You need to step outside into the sculpture gardens and landscaped deer park to get your breath back.

---

*Further Reading*

Barley, M.W., *Lincolnshire and the Fens* (Batsford; London, 1952).

Yates, J. and H. Thorold, *Lincolnshire; A Shell Guide* (Faber and Faber; London, 1965)

*The Madness of King George* (MGM; 1994). The film centres upon Dr Willis and the king and gives a good portrayal of the state of doctoring and psychiatry at that time.

www.themomentmagazine.com

# BINGO AND BIRDING
## Skegness and Gibraltar Point

### INTRODUCTION

This walk from Skegness, out to Gibraltar Point National Nature Reserve and back, offers a taste of two kinds of wildlife. In the depths of winter the walk to the point is a true wilderness experience, especially if there is a squally wind whipping in from the North Sea. In summer it can be even wilder in town, with crowds of holidaymakers hell-bent on having a good time. The walk explores 'Skeggy's' rich heritage as a seaside resort before crossing the dunes to sample the equally rich diversity of wildlife to be found on the reserve.

This offers few difficulties as it basically follows the coast out and back, but be mindful of Greenshank Creek, which should be passed landward if the tide is high. The cafe and reserve centre make an excellent mid-point break. If you don't want to walk out and back (around 8 miles), options are to explore town and nature reserve separately and spend a day exploring each end. This is a useful compromise with the children – 'today we walk, tomorrow we party' (or vice versa). The short walk around the

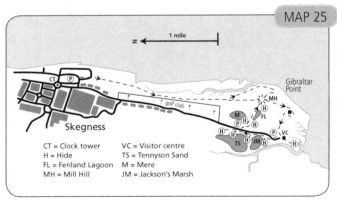

MAP 25

Gibraltar Point

Skegness

CT = Clock tower    VC = Visitor centre
H = Hide    TS = Tennyson Sand
FL = Fenland Lagoon    M = Mere
MH = Mill Hill    JM = Jackson's Marsh

reserve is about 3 miles in all but can take all day if you are birding and beachcombing. One other good option is to get a taxi from Skegness to the point and walk back or vice versa. This is a Grade 3 in fine weather, but 4 in a stiff wind off the sea, as it can be quite exposed.

## TIDES

The tides here can race in and out at great speed, so it is as well to check these first. If you intend to linger and walk out any distance from the shore, then make sure you set off on an outgoing tide and turn back well before the tide turns.

## SKEGNESS TOWN

The Romans had a fort here commanding the Wash, which was considerably narrower in those days, but it now lies underwater. Later the Vikings made a settlement here and eventually Skegness grew into a small port and fishing village, but it was the coming of the railway which brought Skegness fame as a holiday resort, taking advantage of its fine sandy beaches. It is a typical English seaside resort, boasting donkeys, fish and chips, sticks of rock, beaches and amusement arcades. A testament to its popularity is the fact that there are probably more caravans in Skegness than houses. It used to boast a pier over a third of a mile long at 1,843 feet and one could get steamboat trips across the Wash to Hunstanton in Norfolk. However, over the years, drifting ships and severe gales have seriously reduced the pier's length, so much that it now rarely meets the high tide.

## What's in a Name?

Arguably Skegness means 'headland of the bearded one'. The name is in two parts, 'Skeg' and 'Ness'. Ness means headland and if you look at the map of Lincolnshire it is clear to see that Skegness is a headland and the furthest east point in the county. Some sources suggest that Skeg derives from the Norse 'skegg', meaning beard. The Vikings were prolific invaders of Lincolnshire and it is assumed that one such bearded invader established a settlement here and thus the name was born. I wonder what he would think of the modern, tongue-in-cheek 'Skegvegas'! Apparently, back in 1776, a certain Mr John Bynge called it a 'vile, shabby bathing place'! However, because of its flatness and pure air quality, many convalescent homes were set up in Skegness especially for ailing miners from Nottinghamshire and Derbyshire.

## The Jolly Fisherman

This happy, skipping, pipe-smoking fisherman was painted by John Hassell in 1908 and it was bought by the Great Northern Railway to advertise trips to Skegness from King's Cross. The company added the slogan 'Skegness is SO bracing' to highlight the healthy air quality, due to the fact that chilly-north easterly winds often blow in off the North Sea. In 1908 it cost 3 shillings (15p) for a return trip. The fares have increased but the Jolly Fisherman is still the Skegness mascot. The original poster is in the town hall but there is a modern, pipeless and less rotund statue near the clock tower.

## The Clock Tower

This was built in 1899 to commemorate the diamond jubilee of Queen Victoria. It is 56 feet high with a clock on each of its four faces. Each clock is 4 feet across and the tower has a serious list; see if you can notice it! Legend has it that one night, when worse for drink, someone climbed a ladder and put the clocks hands back an hour. This caused considerable mayhem the day after, when many people arrived an hour late at their boarding houses for their midday meal.

## Butlin's Holiday Camp

Whilst not visited upon this walk, it is nonetheless worth saying a few words about how Butlin's helped to put Skegness firmly on the holidaymaker's map. This was Billy Butlin's first camp and was built upon 200 acres of turnip field. Opened in 1936, with all meals and entertainment inclusive, it was designed to be an affordable working man's holiday. It was hugely successful, with its redcoats helping to get everyone to join in the fun, with cries such as 'Good morning, campers'. Bathing beauty, glamorous granny and knobbly knees competitions also abounded, fostering a sense of togetherness. At its height it accommodated up to 10,000 holidaymakers and had a monorail and chairlift, as well as the usual attractions of theatre, swimming pool and amusements. Ringo Starr played here with his band, Rory Storm and the Hurricanes, in 1962 and many famous entertainers cut their teeth as redcoats, here such as Dave Allan and Terry Scott. During the war, Butlin's was used as a training base for the navy and renamed HMS *Royal Arthur*, the dance hall becoming the armoury.

## 1953 FLOODS

The night of 31 January 1953 brought with it the East Coast's worst disaster. A combination of gales and a high tide enabled the sea to breach the sea walls, causing devastation all down the East Coast from Lincolnshire to Essex. Forty-three people died along the Lincolnshire coast and thousands were evacuated, including the entire population of Mablethorpe, amid scenes reminiscent of the war years. Hundreds of acres of farmland were flooded and hundreds of animals died.

## CHURCH FARM MUSEUM

If time permits, visit this museum as it has many traditional Lincolnshire buildings such as farm cottages furnished as in olden times, including the kitchen range. Often staff dress in period costume, so if possible coincide your visit with one of their 'life as it was' special events.

## GIBRALTAR POINT

The route from the seafront at Skegness, out along the dunes and sea lavender-covered mudflats to Gibraltar Point, was one often taken by Tennyson in his youth. We should be grateful that the area is now a National Nature Reserve preserving the wildlife, as there is much to see here. Gibraltar Point, or 'Gib' as it is known, consists of two ridges of sand dunes with saltmarsh in between and mudflats, more saltmarsh and a wide sandy shore on the seaward side.

In the eighteenth century the west dunes used to be the shore, but they are now at least a kilometre from the sea. Many of the higher dunes are colonised by sea buckthorn which, with its profusion of orange berries, gives good cover and food for the birds.

Come here in the autumn and you will see large flocks of thrushes, such as fieldfares, gorging on the berries, having just migrated from Scandinavia.

# Kids' Stuff

**WATCH:**
**The illuminations.** Early autumn is a good time to do this walk because you can combine migration birdwatching with Skegness illuminations, which last until the end of October. It is an excellent excuse for an overnight stay, but you will need to book your accommodation well in advance.

**TRY:**
**Birdwatching.** The target is twenty different species before you get to the visitor centre. Write this up when you get home and send it to the Lincolnshire Wildlife Trust.

**Beachcombing.** Pick up samples of as many objects as you can, such as seaweed, feathers, dogfish and whelk egg cases, seaweed, unusual pebbles, etc. Then, back at home, set about identifying them all.

**PLAY:**
**I Spy.** Prizes for the first to spot: the Jolly Fisherman, redshank, clock tower, oystercatcher, sea buckthorn, pier, rabbit droppings, candy dummy, ghost train and a stick of rock with your name in it.

**The amazing amusement arcade game.** You cannot visit Skeggy without losing some money in the arcades and slot machines. This is the most enjoyable way to lose it! Each person is given £2 in 2p coins and watches are synchronised. At the word 'Loser' each person begins trying to win. After 30 minutes time is called and the person with the most money left wins whatever is left! If everyone has lost everything well in advance of the half hour then fear not as this is normal!

**MAKE:**
**Your parents wet!** It is obligatory that all parents on this walk must go on the wettest ride in the amusement park.

Along the shore you will discover many birds, such as waders and gulls, at all seasons, but it makes for a bracing and interesting autumn walk when migration is in full swing. On some days literally thousands of birds can pass through and 'Gib' becomes a Mecca for birdwatchers looking for rarities that only occur on passage. In spring, exhausted migrants can literally drop out of the sky as they reach first landfall. Breeding birds include redshank and ringed plover, but in winter watch out for the sanderlings: tiny white waders scurrying along the shoreline after food. Out on the saltmarsh you can find the succulent plant samphire which is edible and often called sea asparagus. Gathered in spring, it can be eaten as a salad or pickled in vinegar. Also in spring you will often see skylarks flying about the saltmarsh where they breed. Look out too for the curlew, with its mournful cry and long down-curved bill.

The visitor centre and cafe make a perfect mid-walk break. A short way down the River Steeping, which enters the sea here, lies the once busy port of Wainfleet. When the river silted up, boats could only get as far as the area around the visitor centre and a small community thrived here for a while, with its own pub, the Ship Inn. However, with the ever south-shifting sands, even this silted up in the 1920s and prevented the boats from gaining access. On some parts of the coast, such as the east coast of Yorkshire to the north, the sea is eroding the coast and cliffs at an alarming rate. In other areas, such as here, it deposits its silt and sand. The Point is ever-growing southwards, across the mouth of the Wash, trying to cut off the Steeping's exit.

The River Steeping incidentally, begins life as Tennyson's Brook near Somersby. In the other direction, on a clear day, looking across the Wash from the visitor centre you can see Norfolk about 12 miles away.

---
*Further Reading*

Wright, J., *Skegness at War* (self-published, available from the Jews House bookshop, Steep Hill, Lincoln). This is the home of the Society for Lincolnshire History and Archaeology and is a great source of heritage literature.

www.jollyfisherman.co.uk

www.ssplprints.com

www.lincstrust.org.uk

www.bbc.co.uk/lincolnshire/asop/places/floods/

www.britishpathe.com/video/lincolnshire-flooding

# CROWLAND
## A Taste of the Fens

This 9-mile walk begins at the magnificent ruin of Crowland Abbey and wanders through the town and out along the River Welland to St Guthlac's cross. It returns via an embankment, besides a drain underneath some huge skies. Some will argue that this is a bleak, featureless landscape, but it harbours its own stark beauty. There is parking in the street at Crowland

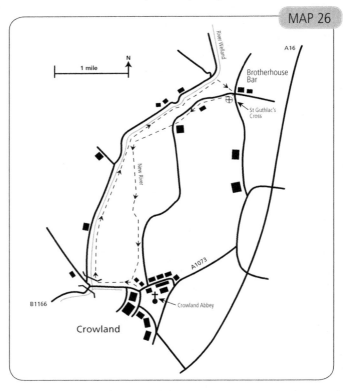

MAP 26

1 mile

N

River Welland

A16

Brotherhouse Bar

St Guthlac's Cross

New River

A1073

B1166

Crowland Abbey

Crowland

and the walk is flat and easy-going. It is a Grade 2 on a fine day but a Grade 4 when the weather blows up.

## CROWLAND AND THE FENS

Crowland is basically built, like Ely its fenland cousin, on an island higher than the surrounding marsh and so is less prone to flooding. This island served as a refuge for St Guthlac, who one can imagine coming upon it out of the mist in his small boat. There was much land reclaimed in the twelfth and thirteenth century, by monks whose monasteries held large flocks of sheep on the rough grassland. The wool was exported via the Wash ports, such as Boston.

The seventeenth century saw the beginning of drainage in earnest, with many locals opposed to it, alongside the Enclosure movement. Livelihoods were at stake but five rivers, including the Welland, drain into the Wash and so the underlying soil is rich with silt deposits. Resistance prevailed for a while but frequent floods, alongside sheep and cattle disease in the early eighteenth century, saw windmills and sluice gates multiply. With advances in technology, some wonderful steam-driven pumps were put into action to divert the water.

In the seventeenth to nineteenth centuries, travel in the Fens was made quite unpleasant by mosquitoes giving travellers marsh fever. At the time it was thought to be caused by the murk of marsh fogs and the local remedy for this 'ague', as it was known, was opium! Locally grown white opium poppies were used and pubs often served beer laced with it. The disease was of course malaria, which literally means bad air ('mal' 'aria'). There was a lot of stagnant water in the Fens, giving the mosquitoes an ideal breeding ground.

One cannot leave this here without exploring some other Lincolnshire remedies. Ketteringham gives us a ring made from a coffin hinge to ward off cramp, moss from a human skull taken as snuff to ward off a headache, sucking a frog to death to get rid of a sore throat and passing the hand of an executed criminal nine times over a swelling to reduce it. We will have to take their word on these, as I have not tried them due to difficulty sourcing the ingredients.

In the seventeenth-century Civil Wars, most of the Fens were Parliamentarian but Crowland remained staunchly Royalist. In 1643, locals armed themselves with scythes and pitchforks and, led by their vicar, resisted the advances of Cromwell's Parliamentarians who had already taken Lincoln. Cromwell's New Model Army eventually prevailed but the Crowland 'affair' highlighted the stubborn resistance of Lincolnshire fensmen, a quality they arguably still retain.

Crowland Bridge, Nr. Peterboro'

The most unusual feature of Crowland is the late fourteenth-century three-arched Trinity Bridge. This was built by monks and used to span two streams of the Welland, which have long since disappeared underground. On one of the flights of steps is a seated figure; some say it represents Christ or the Virgin Mary, while others believe it to be King Ethelbald holding a loaf of bread, and it is said to have been taken from the west front of the abbey. The bridge remained important even after the streams had gone, as it used to be the point at which men gathered every day to be hired to work on the land.

## CROYLAND ABBEY

Croyland is the old form of Crowland and basically means muddy land. The Benedictine abbey retains this spelling and was founded in 716 by a future Mercian king called Ethelbald. This was in gratitude for being helped by St Guthlac, who gave up a military life to become a monk and had lived here as a hermit since 699.

The first abbey was made of wattle and thatch and the abbey has been burnt down and sacked three times. Around 870 the Vikings changed tack from pillaging to wanting to conquer and settle, and in doing so destroyed the early monastery and slayed the abbot at the altar. A fire destroyed the next abbey in 1091 and the partially rebuilt and roofless monastery was destroyed in an earthquake in 1118.

Then came Henry VIII. Before the Black Death, Lincolnshire and the Fens had more monasteries than anywhere else in England. Most were destroyed by Henry VIII's dissolution, but some parishes were allowed to keep part of the monastery to serve as a church, such as Croyland. However, Barley, quoting a contemporary traveller, tells us that it was 'Pillaged to the bone'. In fact, Henry destroyed the choir, transept, tower and many monastic buildings. Much of the stone was, however, recycled and Rogers quotes another contemporary source as saying 'you can see pieces of it in every house'. Check for yourselves! The last 'sacking' was a bombardment by Cromwell in 1643 in response to the town's Royalist leanings. Most of what remains dates from the fourteenth century, but even as a ruin it is a sight to behold, particularly in early morning mist.

The beautiful west front is the best remnant, with its tiers of statues of saints and kings. See if you can spot St Guthlac holding a whip! Below these, above the door of the nave, is a quatrefoil depicting Guthlac's life.

The north aisle remains as the parish church. When inside, make sure to notice the fine roof bosses and the finely carved chancel screen, with the small carving of Guthlac in his boat.

The large Norman font could hold 25 gallons and was used for 'immersion' baptisms. Take a look at the many interesting gravestones as you wander around the ruins and try to find the grave of a Mr Girdlestone, who tried to walk 1,000 miles in 1,000 hours for a bet. He narrowly failed. Notice, too, the dog-toothing on the lonely Norman arch at the far end of the ruined nave. That it still stands is a fine testament to its stonemasons.

# Kids' Stuff

## DRAW:
**The Crowland ruins.** Sit a short while among the ruins and sketch them. Many of our finest watercolour painters, like Turner, spent hours sketching ruins like these.

## MAKE:
**The Crowland ruins.** Bring your drawing to life by creating a papier mâché model complete with grass and sheep

**A silhouette 360-degree horizon.** When you are in the middle of nowhere, take out your sketchpad and draw a line across the middle to represent ground level. Find a reference point such as tree or building and start to draw the horizon. Keep on and on, turning around as you do it, until you get back to your starting point. When you get home, black it in and cut it out to remind you of your walk.

## PLAY:
**Cloud hunting.** Use charts to identify as many clouds as you can: www. wvscience.org/clouds/Cloud_Key.pdf and www.metoffice.gov.uk/media/pdf/r/f/cloud-spotting.pdf.

## LOOK UP:
**The Guthlac Roll.** This is believed to have been drawn by monks at Crowland Abbey in late twelfth century and depicts the life of St Guthlac.

**More gruesome remedies.** Do an Internet search to find more horrible cures.

As you leave Crowland towards the River Welland, notice the long pond on the left of the road which provides a fine foreground to the white water tower ahead.

## BIG SKIES

The flatness of the landscape means that the sky takes up a much larger part of your field of view than normal and is the reason that Lincolnshire has such 'big skies'. We have become used to living and working in enclosed spaces, so this walk along the embankments gives you a real sense of space and openness. You will come back refreshed but consider the weather forecast, as there are few places to hide out here! The beautiful can be very quickly transformed into the bleak.

## GUTHLAC'S CROSS

This is most likely Anglo-Saxon and is a boundary stone marking the limits of the lands of Crowland Abbey. The Latin inscription reads, 'This rock, I say, is Guthlac's utmost bound'.

On the way back along the drain in the summer coot, moorhen, mute swan, heron, reed and sedge warbler and skylark will be your constant companions.

───────────────────────────────────────── *Further Reading*

Barley, M.W., *Lincolnshire and the Fens* (Batsford; London, 1952)
*Croyland Abbey Official Guide* (available at the abbey and well worth a read)
Ketteringham, J.R., *A Lincolnshire Hotchpotch* (J.R. Ketteringham; Lincoln, 1989)
Rogers, A., *A History of Lincolnshire* (Phillimore; Chichester, 1985)
Yates, J. and H. Thorold, *Lincolnshire; A Shell Guide* (Faber and Faber; London, 1965)
lincoln.ourchurchweb.org.uk
www.en.wikipedia.org/wiki/Guthlac_of_Crowland

# A HAVEN FOR BIRDS

## Boston and the Wash

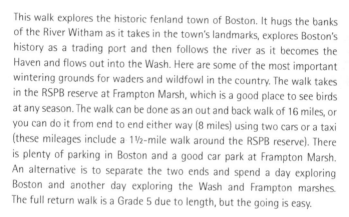

This walk explores the historic fenland town of Boston. It hugs the banks of the River Witham as it takes in the town's landmarks, explores Boston's history as a trading port and then follows the river as it becomes the Haven and flows out into the Wash. Here are some of the most important wintering grounds for waders and wildfowl in the country. The walk takes in the RSPB reserve at Frampton Marsh, which is a good place to see birds at any season. The walk can be done as an out and back walk of 16 miles, or you can do it from end to end either way (8 miles) using two cars or a taxi (these mileages include a 1½-mile walk around the RSPB reserve). There is plenty of parking in Boston and a good car park at Frampton Marsh. An alternative is to separate the two ends and spend a day exploring Boston and another day exploring the Wash and Frampton marshes. The full return walk is a Grade 5 due to length, but the going is easy.

## BOSTON

Boston is regarded as the 'Capital of the Fens' and it lies upon the Greenwich Meridian just like the 'Capital of the Wolds', Louth. The name Boston is said to mean 'St Botolph's town', and Botolph's name was said to mean 'boat help'. A Saxon missionary monk called Botolph was said to have preached here and founded a church on the banks of the Witham in AD 654. A settlement grew up around the church, known as Botolph's Stone, but it was not until Tudor times that Botolph's Stone became Boston. There is some speculation involved here, as some argue that the Witham would not have flowed here in these times.

Boston was growing into a thriving port in the eleventh and twelfth centuries because, with so few good roads, the rivers were the best way of transporting goods. By the beginning of the thirteenth century it had built up a significant trade with Europe and the town received its first

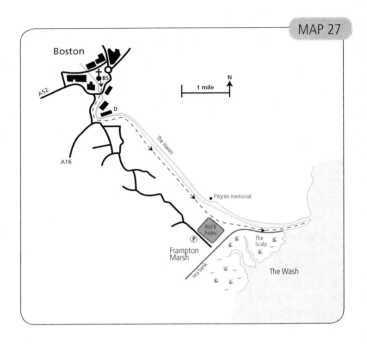

MAP 27

Boston

A52

BS

D

The Haven

1 mile

N

Pilgrim memorial

RSPB hides

P

Frampton Marsh

A16

sea bank

The Scalp

The Wash

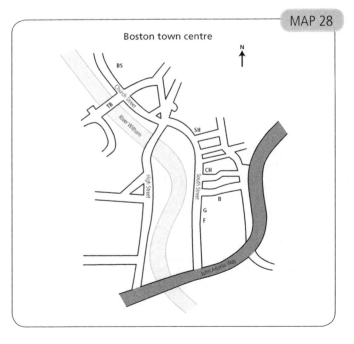

MAP 28

Boston town centre

N

BS

Church Street

TB

River Witham

SH

CH

B

High Street

South Street

G

F

John Adams Way

charter from King John in 1204. From the thirteenth to the fifteenth century, Boston was one of the principal ports in medieval Britain, sometimes handling more trade than London. The bulk of the early trade was in Lincolnshire wool, exported to weavers, particularly in Flanders, and Boston is said to have been built on wool.

Along with the good times, Boston also suffered many devastating floods and fires and the plague wiped out a third of the population in 1348 and a fifth again in the late 1580s. Despite all this, the town grew, with friaries being established by Carmelites, Franciscans, Dominicans and Augustinians. The size of St Botolph's is testament to the wealth of the town at this time.

The wool trade began to decline in the late fifteenth century, with many rich merchants leaving the town. The river was also silting up with sand and mud washed down from the Yorkshire coast. By the eighteenth century, work had begun on draining the Fens to the worry of many locals, whose livelihood depended on wildfowling. Rivers were straightened and embanked to make them navigable and barges ferried people between market towns, picking up goods from the villages bound for Boston Market. In 1884, a new dock and wharves on the Haven were constructed and by the twentieth century, Boston was once again a busy trading port, exporting grain and fertiliser and importing timber. It had a significant fishing fleet too, many of whose trawlers were sunk in the First World War.

## St Botolph's Church (BS)

St Botolph's church (or the 'Stump' as it is called locally) is the largest parish church in England at 282 feet long and 272½ feet high. It also has one of the tallest towers, visible for miles across the Fens and out to sea. Building began in 1309 and continued through the whole reign of Edward III, but the

The Stump, Boston.

tower was built over 100 years later. It is so much a symbol of the prosperity of the town at the time that it is said to be made of wool.

The church has many superb features worthy of close inspection, not the least being the choir stalls and misericords which prove that religion and humour mix well together. The misericords seldom feature religious themes, depicting amusing carvings, such as a jester squeezing a cat and biting its tail, as if it were a set of bagpipes. I particularly like the one with the hunter returning home without any game being assaulted by his wife ... it strikes a chord!

The ceiling was restored in the 1930s, with money raised locally and this is reflected in the roof bosses which depict subjects from Boston's history. One, for example, depicts a white elephant, telling us that it was paid for from the proceeds of a white elephant stall. There are also some fine memorials including some to the Fydell family, those who sailed with Captain Cook to Australia and to the Pilgrims. There is also some impressive stained glass, such as the 'Ladies Window' which commemorates four famous locals, Anne of Bohemia, Margaret Beaufort, Anne Bradstreet and Jean Ingelow.

One particularly fine time to view the interior is when the sun is setting and shining straight through the west window. There are also some fine stained-glass windows with representations of both the 'Stump' itself and Lincoln Cathedral in the marvellous Cotton Chapel.

Martineau calls the church a 'calendar in stone': there are fifty-two windows in the church (one for every week), 365 steps in the tower (days in a year), seven doors (days in the week), and twenty-four steps to the library (hours in the day). As for minutes, there are sixty steps to the roof.

The crowning glory is the tower, described by Daniel Defoe around 1725 as a 'noble and lofty structure' and by Thorold and Yates in 1966 as 'in the style of Bruges but more graceful'. Stand in the middle of this 40 square feet of amazement and look up. It has a vaulted roof 137 feet above with a central boss depicting the 'Agnus Dei' which is reputed to weigh 6 tons. Climb the steep spiral staircase, counting the steps, and you will have a magnificent view of the town and fens below, not to mention the Wash. You can see Lincoln Cathedral from the tower on a clear day some 32 miles distant and Hunstanton across the Wash in Norfolk. The tower is crowned with a sixteenth-century lantern, which may have been lit as a marker for those out at sea.

This is a great place to listen to choral works, especially those of John Tavener, the sixteenth-century composer who is buried under the tower and has a floor memorial. So try and co-ordinate the walk with a concert, which will also give you an excuse for an overnight stay and a chance to visit some of the local brewery Batesmans pubs.

## Town Bridge (TB)
Built in 1913, replacing an iron bridge of 1806. Walk on to it for the views of the Stump back upriver.

## Shodfriars Hall (SH)
This was built in the fifteenth century, most likely as a guildhall. Its three stories and timber frame were heavily restored in 1874, leaving little of the original building.

## Custom House (CH)
Built in 1725, this is a fine example of eighteenth-century architecture constructed to cope with an increase in smuggling.

## Blackfriars Arts Centre (B)
This is the refectory of a thirteenth-century Dominican friary. They were known as Shodfriars because they wore sandals rather than walk barefoot. It was converted into a theatre in 1965.

## Guildhall Museum (G)
This building dates from roughly 1390. It was the base for the Guild of St Mary, which comprised of the local rich and powerful. In 1546 it became the town hall. It is said that Pilgrim Fathers Bradford and Brewster were held here in 1607 before their trial in Lincoln. Be sure to study the fine miniature coastscapes of Boston and the marshes by the local painter William Bartol Thomas. Thomas was born in Boston in 1877, lived here with his sister until his death in 1947 and had a passion for painting the Lincolnshire coast. Also make sure you see the original charter given to the town by Henry VIII in 1545.

ANNE BRADSTREET ⊠    ⊠ JEAN INGELOW

### Fydell House (F)
Built in the 1700s and bought by Joseph Fydell in 1726. He was a textile merchant who twice became the town mayor.

### Route Guidance
The route from here crosses the busy John Adams Way (locally known as the Boston car park) and continues down High Street until you meet the River Witham again. You pass the swing bridge and South Forty-Foot Drain then turn left out along the banks of the Haven.

### Swing Bridge
This is a Grade II listed bridge, built by Handysides iron foundry in Derby in 1882 to connect the docks with the Great Northern Railway.

### Bridge Over South Forty-Foot Drain
The South Forty-Foot Drain is 32 kilometres long and part of a network draining hundreds of square miles of fen, making it suitable for agricultural use. The levels are lowered in winter to help this.

### Boston Docks (D)
All sorts of lifting gear, gantrys and cranes adorn the docks, and the port handles such commodities as grain, fertiliser, animal feeds and metal.


## HAVEN

This is the straightened tidal outfall of the River Witham as its flows out of Boston and into the Wash. The river here used to meander on its way to the Wash and often got silted up, stopping shipping reaching the docks. The Grand Sluice was built in 1766 to regulate the water and scour out the Haven and the river was straightened out between 1800 and 1884, shortening it by some 4 miles. Our scenic walk now takes you past a large landfill site much beloved by gulls and birdwatchers. The path here can get a bit overgrown and indistinct, but the reward for perseverance is well worth it.

### Pilgrim Fathers Memorial
This is halfway along the Haven on the opposite bank and was erected in 1957. It commemorates the place where the pilgrims were arrested as they made their first attempt to leave for Holland in 1607, but were instead betrayed by the captain of the Dutch ship they had chartered. The Pilgrim Fathers were a group of puritans from Nottinghamshire who felt that England was becoming more and more ungodly and wanted to leave so that they could worship as they pleased. They were brought before the

court in the Guildhall but released after a few months. They set sail for the Netherlands, but some found life there too liberal and eventually sailed to the 'new world' in the *Mayflower* in 1620.

## FRAMPTON MARSH AND THE WASH

The Wash used to be much further inland than it is today, but silt washed down from the Yorkshire coast has pushed the coastline further and further eastwards as it gets deposited on the Lincolnshire coastline. Banks have been built to keep out the sea since Roman times and saltmarsh has been reclaimed as farmland over the centuries. Many villages and towns, such as Wainfleet, used to be on the coast but are now some miles from the sea. The rich intertidal sand, mudflats and saltmarsh of the Wash make it internationally important as a migration feeding ground and as wintering quarters for a wealth of wildfowl. There are important saltmarsh plants including sea lavender, sea aster and sea purslane, and the largest common seal colony in Europe.

The RSPB reserve adds freshwater lagoons, wet grassland and a reedbed to an already exciting habitat. Its trails bring you as close as is possible to a remarkable range of bird species and is well worth a walkabout. The volunteers and wardens will help you out with any identification problems which, with waders and wildfowl, can be tricky in times of moult and winter plumage.

---

*Further Reading*

Baldwin, M., 'A Miscellany of Old Lincolnshire', *Lincolnshire Life Magazine* (Dec 1966, Vol. 6, No. 10)

Defoe, D., *1724–6 A Tour Through the Whole Island of Great Britain* (London; Penguin classics, 1986)

Yates, J. and H. Thorold, *Lincolnshire: A Shell Guide* (London; Faber and Faber, 1965)

Martineau, H.D., 'A Cameo of Boston', *Lincolnshire Life Magazine* (1967)

# Kids' Stuff

**DESIGN:**

**A misericord.** Use it to represent all that is important to you; if you had to be remembered by this seat, what would the carvings be of?

**PLAY:**

**Blind recognising.** This is a brilliant thing to do whenever the opportunity arises, and in Boston Stump the opportunity arises often. Look for carvings in stone or wood and when you spot one tell your friend to shut their eyes, then guide their hands onto the carving and get them to try and guess what it is. This gets you in touch with your tactile side. It works equally well with natural objects, such as twigs and plants in a wood.

**Birdwatching.** There are twenty to see: shelduck, oystercatcher, brent goose, dunlin, golden plover, redshank, lapwing, black-headed gull, skylark, teal, curlew, tree sparrow, reed bunting, kestrel, heron, little egret, shoveller, avocet, pied wagtail, herring gull .

**FIND:**

**Tattershall Castle.** Look from the top of the Stump. A prize is awarded to the first person who can see Tattershall Castle.

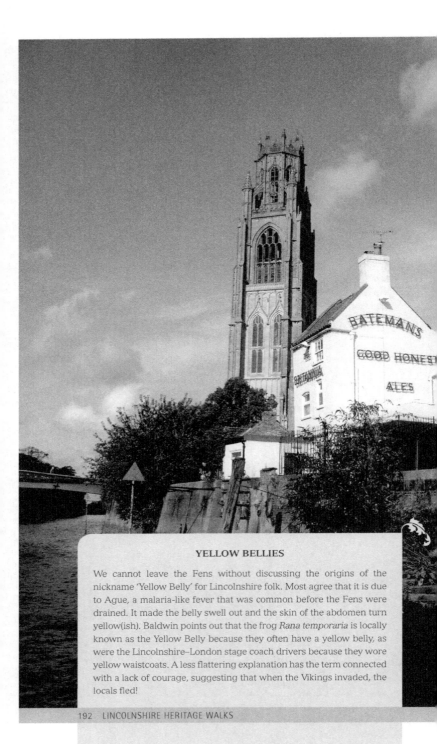

### YELLOW BELLIES

We cannot leave the Fens without discussing the origins of the nickname 'Yellow Belly' for Lincolnshire folk. Most agree that it is due to Ague, a malaria-like fever that was common before the Fens were drained. It made the belly swell out and the skin of the abdomen turn yellow(ish). Baldwin points out that the frog *Rana temporaria* is locally known as the Yellow Belly because they often have a yellow belly, as were the Lincolnshire–London stage coach drivers because they wore yellow waistcoats. A less flattering explanation has the term connected with a lack of courage, suggesting that when the Vikings invaded, the locals fled!